BON JOVI

RUNAWAY

BON JOVI

RUNAWAY

Dave Bowler and Bryan Dray

B◈XTREE

Published in Great Britain in 1995 by
Boxtree Limited,
Broadwall House, 21 Broadwall, London SE1 9PL.

Front cover design: Shoot That Tiger!

Front cover photos: Redferns

Picture credits

NE/Geronimo/Redferns: page 2 *bottom*
Mick Hutson/Redferns: pages 3, 4
Ebet Roberts/Redferns: pages 1; 2 *top left and right*

Typeset by SX Composing Limited, Rayleigh, Essex
Printed by Redwood Books, Trowbridge, Wiltshire

ISBN 0 7522 0760 1

10 9 8 7 6 5 4 3 2 1

A CIP catalogue is available from
the British Library.

CONTENTS

DEDICATION

To Mom and Dad
Grace under pressure. Thank you.
And for Denise
And though you hold the keys to ruin . . .
Always

David

To Trish, Emma and Rebecca
For their constant love and support.
And Mum, Dad, Gran, Joyce and Wal.
For all their help.

Bryan

Acknowledgments

In the production of any book a number of people other than ourselves are unfortunate enough to be involved. Foremost among these are all at the Tanja Howarth Agency. Further invaluable assistance came from Boxtree.

A lot of the research was carried out at the National Sound Archive which provides superb facilities (and deserves considerably more government funding than it receives). Denise Dean did far more of that research than was entirely wise and for that we are extremely grateful. Thanks also to Tracy Jenkins for the loan of some extra material.

Thanks are also due to Dublin's legendary *Hot Press*, *Q*, *Select*, *Melody Maker*, *Vox*, *Sounds*, *Raw*, *Kerrang!*, *Record Mirror*, *Smash Hits* and *New Musical Express* for granting permission to quote from their extensive files. Thanks also to Evelyn Bernal for permission to reproduce quotes from *Rolling Stone*, reprinted by permission of Straight Arrow Publishers, Inc. 1989, all rights reserved. Details of all the relevant articles used appear in the sources section at the back of the book.

Finally for anyone desperately seeking other Bon Jovi fans, send a large SAE to Kate at Midlands Metal International, 47 Thackeray Walk, Stafford, Staffordshire ST17 9SE.

INTRODUCTION

It can't have escaped many people's notice that over the past decade, Bon Jovi have been among the most successful artists in the world. Jon Bon Jovi is at the heart of that triumph and is one of the most familiar faces in popular music today. Certainly few of his contemporaries have appeared with such regularity in the tabloid as well as the music press and few people with even the most passing interest in popular culture would have any trouble in recognizing the face that stares down from a million bedroom walls across the globe.

Although Bon Jovi is presented to the world as a band in the fullest sense of the term, there's little question that it is Jon Bon Jovi who calls the tune. The group carries his name, Polygram's recording contract is with him alone, he decides when they'll write, record and tour. If Richie Sambora is a particularly important component in the writing process, it is still Jon's talents that come to the fore, his image that helps sell the records, his charismatic personality which has shaped the group, built an audience and filled stadiums. As their respective solo records illustrate, it is Jon Bon Jovi who is the populist force within their hierarchy while Sambora's commercial following is considerably smaller.

The outstanding commercial success of Bon Jovi was a story peculiar to the 1980s. Constructed on the foundations of a video-friendly image that helped to define MTV, coupled with some unpretentious and determinedly commercial tunes, everything about the group suggested a preordained masterplan that would countenance nothing short of multi-platinum sales. Jon Bon Jovi, the archetypal rock'n'roll runaway, had his own dreams very clearly in focus throughout the decade. Musically he was intent on delivering the good time sound-track to a decade of self-indulgence where the acquisition of wealth seemed to be society's cornerstone. He had the working man's understanding that financial security alone could provide personal and professional freedom, a truism that his hero Bruce Springsteen had embraced before him, albeit with less apparent relish.

Given that Bon Jovi chose to operate in the traditionally conservative arena of hard rock, they were the ideal band for the times. The central topics of girls and good times that have been the genre's staple for many years were the themes of the age. It's difficult to dismiss the idea that Bon Jovi quite deliberately dealt in bold caricatures for maximum commercial advantage given their early influences which were considerably more diverse than albums like *Bon Jovi* and *7800 Degrees Fahrenheit* might suggest. Whatever the case, they were soon immersed in such a dense working schedule that they had little chance to pause for breath and reconsider both achievements and future.

As the 1980s drew to a close, Jon Bon Jovi came up for air. Although the wall upon wall of gold and platinum discs bore testimony to the popularity of his work, the real test of an important artist is their ability to maintain momentum into a second decade, continuing to develop alongside the needs of changing times. Contemporaries U2, who had won equivalent commercial plaudits, stripped down their group to basics and reinvented themselves, adopting new clothes and a new attitude. Coming from a very different area of rock'n'roll, that was never a viable option for Bon Jovi for it would have courted derision. Weathering the Seattle broadside, Jon resolutely refused to dabble in grunge but instead refined Bon Jovi's sound, reassessed his lyrical slant, looked again at his own backyard and emerged as a rather different and highly contemporary musical character.

Other challenges have had to be faced too. Though he would protest, it cannot be denied that much of his success has rested on his photogenic quality, a quality that will inevitably diminish as the years go by. That facet of Bon Jovi's success was reined in to good effect initially with *Blaze Of Glory* and then with the release of *Keep The Faith*. Accordingly, critics began to give the band – and their leader in particular – a little more credit for the work they'd done over the years.

That body of work is consistently strong, if unambitious early on. Jon Bon Jovi is clearly nothing if not smart and little has been left to chance in the development of his band. Like groups such as Def Leppard, he took the hard rock genre as his model and built on the foundations of a new style that Van Halen had already hinted at in cross-over hits such as 'Jump'. Hard rock, together with its close relative heavy metal, was a field that by the late 1970s was apparently inhabited by men with very large egos and commensurate stomachs. By its very nature a form that encouraged excess, many of its practitioners had fallen by the wayside and those that survived were rarely at the peak of physical or mental condition. A lumbering dinosaur, it survived thanks to the fierce loyalty of its fan-base.

It wasn't until the advent of Bon Jovi in particular that the audience expanded to welcome girls into the fold. From their previously subservient role as rock star accessories, young women were now treated as an important part of the audience, while Jon Bon Jovi gave the form its first real sex symbol since Robert Plant's halcyon days. Bon Jovi were such a perfect band for record company demographics that it's hard to imagine that they weren't manufactured in the same way as the Monkees had been to capitalize on The Beatles' audience. The truth is that Jon Bon Jovi did believe in the music that he was making, but that his musical ideals were quickly overtaken by the music industry juggernaut and did not see the light of day again until he took a break.

Bon Jovi may be dismissed as musical lightweights who, in the greater scheme of things, ultimately mean nothing. Certainly their critics seek to do just that, citing enormous sales as evidence that their music is watered down to appeal to the lowest common denominator. It's obvious that the band are unlikely to rank with The Beatles or Hendrix as supreme innovators, but then that could be said of virtually every group around at present. What Jon Bon Jovi has done is entertain a lot of people. He has consistently given of his best and is presently transforming himself into an artist for whom longevity is both intriguing and appealing. With the release of the multi-platinum compilation album *Cross Road*, the first part of his career is at a close. It is a chapter that commands respect and deserves commemoration for it covers one of the greatest success stories of modern musical times.

1

AMERICAN DREAMS

For almost a century now, much of America's popular culture has been built upon or inspired by the notion of the 'American Dream', a shorthand for everything that is held to be of value on that vast continent. If the last fifteen years have provided a better example of those historical threads coming together than in the rise of John Bongiovi, it does not come readily to mind. Bongiovi first saw the light of day on March 2nd 1962 in Perth Amboy, New Jersey, just south of the state border with New York. New Jersey, nicknamed the Garden State, has been no stranger to immigrants over the years, Dutch settlers colonizing it in the 17th century prior to British rule. It was given the statehood in 1787 and became one of the original Thirteen States of the Union. As time has moved on, its proximity to New York has meant that it has taken on an ever-more-cosmopolitan aspect, almost as an overspill from that most densely populated of states. New Jersey itself has a population of around eight million people, whose economic security rests on such diverse products as fruit and vegetables, chemicals, clothing and electrical machinery.

John grew up in Sayreville, another New Jersey town, where his family had moved when he was just four. He and his two younger brothers grew up in a solid, safe environment. The family was not wealthy by any stretch of the imagination but they lived comfortably. As the surname Bongiovi indicates, John came from Italian stock. His father, John senior, was a hairdresser. Like so many of his ilk, he worked hard six days a week to pay the rent and create his own piece of America where his family could grow in material and emotional security. John's mother Carol came from the neighbouring state of Pennsylvania where in her youth she had been a local beauty, being crowned Miss Erie and becoming a Playboy Bunny. Once married, Carol Bongiovi had a number of jobs before she settled to work as a florist to augment the family income.

John's family background has often been overlooked in considering his career, but even the most cursory study of his *modus operandi* in Bon Jovi reveals the influence of an Italian upbringing. Bon Jovi operates as a brotherhood of sorts, illustrating very clearly the enormous emphasis that the Italian people put on family life and values. John's favourite movie is *The Godfather* and it's not hard to see why. In the Bon Jovi organisation, he is Don Bon Jovi, the undisputed head of the musical family, but there is a fierce loyalty to the other members of the troupe. John has never been critical of any member of the group or their one-time management in public and any harsh words that he feels necessary are exchanged behind closed doors. This is a traditional family set-up, that close association overriding any other considerations. These are values that would have been instilled in the young Bongiovi simply from personal experience. Looking back for the *Sunday Times* in 1993, he recalled: 'I look back to mealtimes at home, me sitting there with my two younger brothers, and I always see them as joyful events. Family life in general was very happy.'

Another Italian tradition that John came up against very early on in life was the Roman Catholic church. This was considerably less palatable to the young boy and caused problems as he grew up and reacted angrily to the catechism. Though he didn't go through the everyday adolescent rebellion against his parents who were thoroughly supportive of all his ideas and ambitions, school was completely beyond redemption. He hated the very idea of the place, and by the time he was a senior he confessed that 'I showed up but I wasn't there. I was like a jailbird looking out the window going "fly bird, fly" and thinking of rock'n'roll ... I'd be out of school by noon.'

School itself was bad enough, but the religious teaching he had been forced to endure in his earliest years there left an indelible mark. In the course of the *Cross Road* promotional circus, he informed Q that 'I'm a recovering Catholic. Daily. My whole head is completely fucked with what you're brought up to believe in.' Like most of his peers, his first days at school were coloured by Catholicism and the apparently inevitable guilt conditioning that somehow seems to go with the inculcation of that faith. John admits that even now it's a problem that he wrestles with. The heavy workload that he accepted might have been put down to the Protestant work ethic in the case of other performers, but for John it was a case of coming to terms with a dose of Catholic guilt at his financial good fortune. He refuses to concede the point in interviews but his commitment to raising money for charity and his determination to take his music to his fans and to give them a show to remember indicates one who has never forgotten his roots. He admitted as much to Q when questioned about the Catholic guilt syndrome: 'it's the worst. The fuckin' worst . . . who's to say that Judaism is not the right religion, or Buddhism?'

Religious education clearly got under the skin of the young Bongiovi. Though he was never renowned for being a violent or aggressive child, he was thrown out of his Catholic school for slapping a girl; the only time he has been accused of violence. By the time he reached high school, his parents felt that the time might be right to reintroduce him to the faith but 'I begged them to let me out' he confessed to David Cavanagh. 'I couldn't handle it.' It's probable that this subjection to religious teaching by rote was the origin of his difficulties with authority and establishment figures which marred the rest of his schooling. Faced by what he saw as the absurdity of a religious approach which denied any sense of spirituality, reducing the supposed word of God to petty rules and regulations, Bongiovi found himself more and more drawn to the outsiders in society who had cast off all the restrictions and created another reality for themselves – the cowboys of his favourite films and the rock'n'roll outlaws he loved on record.

Aside from his school expulsion, John Bongiovi's youth is uncontroversial and short of any cathartic or pivotal incident.

Alongside the formative aspects of ordinary family life, John's other great influence was the state of New Jersey itself and the 'Joisey attitude' which he describes thus:

> It's the same kind of attitude that places like Liverpool and Sheffield have and places like London, New York, L.A. and Tokyo don't have. The small town, small state, underdog thing always kept you fighting, kept you looking up, 'cos there wasn't that fashion consciousness . . . a lot of fighters, people chasing their dreams.

Although it has a state border with New York, New Jersey might as well be on the other side of America for the state of mind is so different. New York bears all the hallmarks of an entertainment capital; it's the home of Broadway, Greenwich Village was the haunt of the likes of Bob Dylan back in the sixties, it has a powerful film and television infrastructure and so on. It also prides itself on the highbrow nature of the art it produces when compared with the doggedly populist nature of the west coast – and Hollywood in particular.

Music was the most obvious outlet for anyone interested in creating their own fun, for the Jersey shoreline was peppered with bars where new bands could hang out and try their hand. Appearing in front of a mixed clientele of local workers or people from further afield out for a day at the beach at Asbury Park, as long as they could put on a good rock'n'roll show a group of kids might quickly feel at home in a bar, free from the derision their efforts might earn elsewhere. It was in bars such as these in the sixties that Bruce Springsteen and Southside Johnny took their first faltering steps into the world of rock'n'roll, learning their craft as musicians playing raucous cover versions for the edification of drunken hordes and then, their names and reputations assured, learning how to write songs of their own and how to work a crowd.

Southside and Springsteen were, naturally enough, the heroes that John Bongiovi grew up admiring and wanting to emulate. But of course their apprenticeship was very different in character to the one that John would have to endure. Springsteen, in particular, was a trailblazer, it was he who showed that an ordinary guy from Nowhere, New Jersey could make a record and be a success across America. When Bruce was charting this virgin territory, there was no guarantee that he would be a success, no firm footsteps in which to follow. By virtue of his impressive personality and his towering gifts as a songwriter, Bruce Springsteen was able to carve out an alternative reality for himself, after which he could be cited as a precedent by every up-and-coming youngster with a guitar in his hand.

Bruce Springsteen was not the first popular singer to emerge from New Jersey – a couple of other great over-achievers had emerged from its sprawl over the previous decades in the shape of Paul Robeson, who despite the limited opportunities available to black singers had a hugely successful career until he was forced into political exile in the UK, and the legendary Frank Sinatra. John Bongiovi himself was born closer to Brooklyn than Asbury Park, but the stateline that he would need to cross was a huge psychological barrier, the enforcement of an almost pathological inferiority complex among his peers. Only those who were sufficiently confident in themselves and driven by overweening ambition could cross that artistic line. In rock'n'roll terms, Bruce Springsteen dismissed that complex and therefore paved the way for others in his neighbourhood to follow.

It was the excitement that The Boss and Southside Johnny and his band, the Asbury Jukes, generated that first lured John into the rock'n'roll lifestyle. He had been given a guitar by his mother when he was just seven years old but 'I threw it down the basement stairs. When I was thirteen I asked them for a guitar and they told me to fix the one in the basement with the broken tuning-peg.' This anecdote is doubly significant – firstly it illustrates that while his parents offered John plenty of encouragement in his interests they were just as determined to ensure he took nothing for granted and kept his feet on the ground, a contributory factor in his commendably down-to-earth attitude once Bon Jovi acquired the Midas touch. But it is what he did at the age of thirteen that most reveals what was going on in John's mind. He was thirteen in 1975, the year that Bruce Springsteen released *Born To Run*, an instant classic that took the music world by storm. For John Bongiovi it was a case of perfect timing. Looking for something to do with himself beyond school, music became that central release.

Although the Springsteen comparison are unwelcome to both men, the contrasting careers provide an interesting frame of reference for understanding John's music and motivations. The two have long been compared with one another, erroneously for the most part, for the differences between the two are far more compelling than the similarities.

When John recorded the *Blaze Of Glory* album in 1990, he told reporters that Little Richard, who worked on that record, had been his father's hero. That more than anything else makes the generational gap between John and Bruce Springsteen crystal clear. The thirteen years that separate their respective births coincided with the critical period in rock'n'roll history. It meant that John's father was young enough to appreciate the advent of Elvis and to enjoy the thrill of this primitive but undeniably exciting new form. Springsteen's dad was that much older, became a father before rock exploded, and so treated it with the mixture of contempt and fear common to his generation. Both of John's parents were able to understand their son's attraction to rock music and were happy to encourage him to throw himself into something positive, whereas the stories of the furious fights across the Springsteen table are legion. Springsteen had to make his own way against a background of animosity, John Bongiovi was helped all the way.

John readily acknowledges the debt that he owes to The Boss and Southside Johnny: 'The fiction became reality . . . five or ten miles south from here Johnny was making records, Bruce was making records . . . they'd sing a song about this certain road, it was right out in my back yard . . . that intrigued me, that it could just maybe happen.' Whether John seriously considered the possibilities of making a career in music before these seismic events in the mid-seventies is open to debate. Certainly there was little evidence of any burgeoning talent prior to that time. The only apprenticeship he seemed to take an interest in was the pharmaceutical kind, for he later confessed that 'I started doing drugs at thirteen because all of my friends were doing it and you wanted to fit in . . . I smoked way too much [dope]. My parents thought "Oh my God, our son's a drug addict!"'

As John paid less and less attention to school, he fell in with a pretty rough crowd of older kids who introduced him to acid too, though he later felt that it might have been a blessing in disguise: 'Maybe doing drugs that early prevented me from going wild when my career started taking off . . . that gang life produced a lot of casualties. Most of my friends from that time are dead.' With John dabbling in the seamier side of life, rock'n'roll, that great symbol of rebellion, ironically provided a more wholesome activity which his parents quickly got behind, a further explanation of their complete support for his music. John conceded later that 'I've been playing in bars since I was sixteen, before it was legal for me to drink. We'd play until 3am then I'd go home and have to be in school by 8am. My parents didn't mind. At least they knew where I was.'

Possibly his parents recognized John's potential early on, perhaps they really did have faith in the American Dream as it had been represented to their forebears, or maybe their heads were turned by Springsteen transforming dream into tangible reality, a future that they might have hoped their son could share. More likely they were simply glad to find John taking an interest in something other than drugs, an interest which would take him out of himself for, strange though it might seem, he was an introverted child: 'I've always been a loner . . . I wasn't ever the life of the party.'

By withdrawing and spending time alone he was able to concentrate on plans for the future. He fashioned a powerful sense of purpose, an ability to focus totally on the task in hand allied to enormous reserves of determination and will-power. These were to be the source of the strength which ultimately carried him to commercial viability and then success, though this was still some way in the distance as he was completing school and spending the rest of his time between the beach and the bars. Still, he had been bitten by the music bug which in turn, to his parents' relief, meant that he began to take a little interest in school life. With his first group, Raze, he played a school talent contest – coming last – as well as taking a bit part in the school version of the musical *Mame*. These were still small-scale sidelines but it's apparent that Bongiovi was starting to dream on a larger scale and it's here that he and Springsteen diverge once again.

In so much of his early music, Bruce Springsteen dealt with the real world around him. An album like *Born To Run* was about the struggles that faced young guys like himself trying to make their way in the world. Bruce's lyrics were decidedly blue collar, looking at the problems of raising a family and paying the rent while dreaming of a world beyond that was always out of reach. Springsteen took the lives of his friends and hurled them into his music. He mythologized his New Jersey surroundings, turned everyday life into a compellingly romantic battleground strewn with broken hearts and couples fighting against the insurmountable odds. Bruce's vision of his home state was one of heroic, epic proportions. Instinctively he sympathized with the downtrodden who were unable to break free from the humdrum routine, the friends who, metaphorically at least, he had left behind in the wake of his transformation into The Boss. As a lyricist, Bruce's preoccupations were down to earth and compassionate, always looking to deal in the drama of New Jersey.

John Bongiovi, on the other hand, invested in a different facet of the great dream. Where Springsteen romanticized normality, John turned his thoughts to the glamorous notion of escape, creating a quixotic impression of himself as the archetypal cowboy hero of the movies he'd watched as a child. Though he was probably unaware of it, in so doing he fused together many of the diverse elements that so characterize the notion of the American Dream – the chance to rise above yourself and your surroundings, the determination to grasp opportunities and the pioneering spirit that won the West. In essence he and Springsteen worked from opposite sides of the same coin, Bruce rooted in mundane reality, John projecting himself into everyone's escapist fantasies.

Certainly those contrasting points of view were to create a palpable difference between the work of the two men. Bruce Springsteen has long been described as a musician who cares more about life's losers than its winners and one who, when he encounters the grinding routine of blue collar life, feels that 'there but for the grace of God go I'. While John has remained very close to his roots too, his family and friends ensuring that he has not taken on any airs, his initial motive seemed simply to get a place among those winners. With that distinctive streak of pragmatism that has served Bon Jovi so well, John realized early on that to opt out of the rat-race not only took courage but also regular injections of hard cash. Without the material wherewithal to feed them, ideals can quickly perish. As he was nearing school-leaving age with no interest in, and perhaps little aptitude for, further education, John could see a future stretching before him as a factory worker, trying to earn enough to pay the rent and to go out at weekends. That was no kind of life for him and he channelled that cold determination into leaving those everyday worries behind him and carving out a very different existence. By sheer force of will, John's greatest invention, initially at least, was himself as putative rock star, a leap of the imagination that far outdistanced the songs he was beginning to write.

Paradoxically, his regard for that pioneering spirit and the idea of riding off into the sunset was a factor in shaping the relatively conservative nature of his musical tastes. Inevitably the music that surrounded him in New Jersey had a formative effect on the kind of sounds that appealed, while the likes of the Rolling Stones quickly became heroes too. Given his cowboy fixation, it was more significant that Philip Lynott of Thin Lizzy should become a particular hero; a larger-than-life rocker, Lynott's roguish personality endeared him to men and women alike. Though he was later accused of simply aping Springsteen or Jagger, John's performance and attitude resembled that of Lynott far more closely, a comparison that is generally overlooked.

Like so many of his peers, John's ear was taken by that bar band staple, rhythm'n'blues. Not only was he excited by the music as an observer, but he saw in it a vehicle for his own talents. His lack of regard for bands like Talking Heads – he confessed that he didn't understand them – indicates that he was a populist, keen to play the kind of music that cut across social and intellectual divides and touched people on an instinctive level – but there was more to it than that. R'N'B has historically been the root of most of pop's greatest success stories and Bongiovi would not have been slow to realise that by updating it into a more contemporary style, he might be able to carve out a niche for himself. Certainly there would have been no thought of platinum records, but the feeling was strong that a career in a working band might be well within his compass.

To some, the idea of running away from responsibility and the adoption of a lifestyle beyond the nine-to-five is a means to an end. All that fired John's imagination as a sixteen- or seventeen-year-old was the thought of breaking free of the employment treadmill. Simply knowing that you no longer had to clock on and off at the office or factory was the goal that consumed him; he had no plans more grandiose than avoiding working for a living. By instinct, John Bongiovi was not a rebel, for he was blessed with too much native intelligence and compassion for others to take such a wilfully self-centred course. But he was – and remains, albeit to a lesser degree – a runaway who dedicated himself to a life that could be couched in the romantic terms of an old Wild West hero, an outlaw on the run from society itself.

2

LIFE AT THE FAST LANE

There was a time in the last century when outlaws were people to be feared, men who lived on their wits on the fringes of society, doing what they wanted to do, just how they wanted to do it. Those men were tamed by time and a culture that rejected them as the criminals they were, while still glorifying their deeds in books and then in films. If you wanted to stay inside the law but still needed to jettison the conventions of the workaday world, the romantic ideal was to run away and join the circus. By 1960, the circus had been replaced by the rock'n'roll experience where kids, their heads stuffed with dreams of fame, fortune and no more rules, might go to find their future. School, as Alice Cooper exclaimed, was out forever.

Back in 1975, all John Bongiovi wanted was to escape the clutches of school, the grim conformity and the miserable future that seemed ordained for him. Talking to *Melody Maker* he revealed some of his motivation, the source of his unquenchable desire for success:

My father never saw the world, his father never saw the world. He lived and died in New Jersey. My grandfather was a plumber until it killed him believe it or not. Being a fucking plumber shouldn't kill you. My father cut hair and would've died cutting hair if I hadn't convinced him he didn't have to. That's what the world does to you; you grow up, you get a

15

job, you get married, you have two point two children, a white picket fence, you watch TV at night and go to work five days a week. That's what the real world's all about and I wasn't ready for it.

Escapism really was the key note of John Bongiovi's young life. All he was out for was a good time, all of the time, and the rock'n'roll lifestyle, like the travelling circus before it, seemed to offer the means of release. If the New Jersey background explains some of his musical tastes, this aspect of his personality reinforced his demand for entertainment and has conditioned his approach to his craft as performer and songwriter. Ironically, it is this very dedication to providing his audience with what they want – commercial melodies wrapped up in a rocker's persona – that has led Bon Jovi into the heart of the mainstream and the establishment that they were originally rebelling against. In eschewing any kind of experimentation in their early records, Bon Jovi steered the straightest of courses towards mass acceptance. By doing so, they relinquished any claim they might have had to truly rebellious or subversive credentials, which are what real rock'n'roll is supposed to be about. When he and his group threw themselves into the conventional lifestyle of a band on the road – booze and babes – they were merely endorsing the most conservative of rock'n'roll's core values.

In fairness, John was both instinctively, and by virtue of his upbringing, unashamedly populist and proud of it. We've seen that New Jersey had no time for affectation and that his parents were honest, decent people who liked to enjoy themselves at the end of a working week. To add to that, John's brush with Catholicism – the one true religion, as its adherents like to claim – would have left him with a powerful dislike for exclusivity of any kind. For John, people needed to be brought together, not segregated, and he later argued that the article of his faith was simple: 'I just feel you've got to do right by yourself and other people.'

So while John Bongiovi was not a rebel without a cause, rock'n'roll provided a focus for his adolescent frustrations, and superficially at least it also offered that other great panacea, a chance to get the girls. As a quiet, tongue-tied teenager, John wasn't the ladies' man he was later to become, so playing the guitar gave him a certain kudos that enhanced his burgeoning matinée idol looks. Yet once he got on stage there were no ulterior motives required, for he realized that this was his natural habitat, just as Carl Lewis is only fully alive and at home on the athletics field. The adolescent Bongiovi lived for his music first, with girls running a distant second. Even so, at Sayreville High School, he began a long-running relationship with Dorothea Hurley, a tempestuous on-off affair that was to lead to marriage many years down the line.

He first took to the stage in earnest in bar bands in and around Asbury Park, though prior to that he had played local dances, parties and so on. Cover versions were the inevitable staple – from bands such as Kiss, Aerosmith, Bachman Turner Overdrive and all the other usual suspects – but John was keen to slip in his own compositions in the midst of the set, to reasonable acclaim, indicating that he was moving in the right direction. As noted, his first real show came at high school, fronting Raze, a short-lived combo who had originally taken the rather optimistic title Starz, and who perished when their very obvious limitations were cruelly exposed under the spotlights. But John had already acquired a taste for singing before an audience and started to cast around for another group.

Looking back from his current position at the head of a multi-million dollar organisation, life was ludicrously simple back in the late 1970s, as John told *Select*: 'Then playing the local bar was the coolest thing in the world. Playing a college was the big time. I didn't even know where the continent of Europe was [in 1979]. I would've paid a little more attention in school if I'd known what was gonna happen.' In '78, there was no time to waste on school for far more exciting things were going on in his life including, allegedly, an entrepreneurial spell selling counterfeit posters outside a Springsteen concert at Madison Square Gardens in order to pay for his ticket. 'Rock'n'roll pulled me through my bad times,' he conceded later when trying to find a reason for his lifelong love affair with the form.

It's easy to understand why he became so quickly intoxicated with playing live: 'When I was sixteen I'd ask friends what they did last night and they'd say watched *Dallas*. I'd been jamming with Bruce Springsteen, Edgar Winter, Johnny Winter. The school band I was in would open for anybody.' To reach this plateau of local success, John had taken his place at the front of a ten-piece group called Atlantic City Expressway, or ACE for short. Kicking around formulaic rhythm'n'blues tunes, John found difficulty in getting his colleagues to play original material but persevered, meanwhile enjoying his moment of local stardom.

Timing is so often the crucial ingredient in any success story and so it proved with Bongiovi. A few years later the drinking laws were changed, destroying the thriving club scene in New Jersey; had these laws come earlier, John might never have got the chance to get up on stage. As it was, he found himself learning his trade at the very heart of America's finest finishing school. His young band often had the considerable boost of finding Southside Johnny, Little Steven Van Zandt or even The Boss himself jumping on stage to join in the fun. Springsteen, already one of the most important figures in American rock culture, made nothing of his fame, carried no pretensions and loved nothing more than indulging his passion for hot, sweaty rock'n'roll. By refreshing himself at the source of his initial inspiration, Bruce could return to the more serious battles revitalized without needing to relive his youth on vinyl. Impressed by the natural candour and friendliness of his heroes, John vowed that should success come his way, he would endeavour to follow their example.

The bar circuit was the ideal way of letting off steam for friends looking to make a few dollars playing music, but as Springsteen had shown it could also be a perfect stepping stone towards greater things. That was certainly the way that John's mind was working and he took every opportunity to learn from those that had gone before. ACE's reputation grew in their locale and support slots were forthcoming, as he recounted later: 'Everyone went to The Fast Lane in Asbury Park. I opened for everybody there. It was there that Southside Johnny told me all about Sam Cooke and Springsteen gave me a copy of *The Raspberries Greatest Hits* and said "you'll love this" ... I was 16 or 17, still at school, and I knew Aerosmith!'

Even though John was introduced to the legendary debauchery of Aerosmith at such a tender age, and though by his own admission he was still dabbling in drugs, there was no likelihood that he would go off the rails. Rock'n'roll had lit a fire inside him, such that he felt he had seen his own destiny. With that rare intensity of purpose, he resolved that he would make a life for himself within the music industry and set about the toughest of apprenticeships, covering all the bases and developing a healthy grasp of business politics and finance. The image of a young man stumbling into the music industry is an attractively romantic one, but it's far from the truth. As he told *Sounds* in an early interview, 'I wanted to do this so bad it wasn't a case of "if" only "when". I just wouldn't let anything get in my way.' This is just one of the compelling paradoxes about John Bongiovi – he's extremely businesslike and determined in the way that he conducts his affairs with both his group and his record company and yet he has still managed to retain his childlike enthusiasm for the music itself, an impressive feat when one considers the number of jaded rock musicians who simply go through the motions. One is forced to the conclusion that he really is a rock'n'roller for the joy of it, but that he saw the way in which the likes of Aerosmith were ripped off early in their careers and vowed never to let the same thing happen to him. Having analysed the music corporations, John knew his worth and would not settle for less.

ACE were by all accounts an old-fashioned good time outfit who were popular at parties in a Blues Brothers style, the horn section giving their sound a powerful kick. Ten-piece groups are rarely designed for a long and distinguished career and the band disintegrated almost as quickly as it was formed. Significantly, it was John that was the catalyst of its collapse. He had struck up a close friendship with keyboard player David Bryan Rashbaum, another Jersey boy who was a month older than John. Rashbaum trained classically from the age of seven and for him ACE represented nothing more than a chance to earn a little pocket money while playing a different kind of music. He was a fanatical musician, totally committed to the ideal of becoming a professional, and for him ACE passed the time before he could go on to greater things. As soon as the opportunity presented itself, he enrolled at New York's prestigious Juilliard School with a view to a career in classical music.

With Rashbaum out of the group, the Atlantic City Expressway lost some of its shine for John and he immediately followed his friend's example by quitting the band, an early example of the familial solidarity with which he approaches his closest relationships. Without John's magnetic personality at the head of the line, ACE fell apart almost instantaneously. Though he was still little more than a naive kid, John was more determined than ever to make his way as a singer and performer. Rashbaum's defection gave him pause for thought and he reassessed what he wanted to achieve and how he wanted to get there. A few moments of reflection revealed that ACE was obviously not the best vehicle for those dreams. Unprepared to let that stand in his way, he quit without any anxiety as to the consequences for the rest of the band and was on the look-out for another gig immediately.

One of the most important breaks in his life came when he secured the frontman role in a band called The Rest. They were the brainchild of Jack Ponti, a talented rock songwriter who was later to collaborate with John on 'Shot Through The Heart', the most impressive track on the *Bon Jovi* album. Ponti recognized Bongiovi's talent and impressive personality and quickly installed him as the focal point in The Rest. The spell that John had with this band was significant. The Rest had a solid local following, allowing them to play gigs night after night, providing John with the time and space to experiment as both singer and performer, and learn how to work an audience and pace a show. With the backing of Ponti and a talented group, John absorbed musical lessons and began to exude confidence every time he went on the stage. Safe in the knowledge that the band could almost guarantee a good reception, John wasn't afraid to try new ideas, all the time assembling a powerful armoury of tricks of the showman's trade. In addition, it gave him the reassuring knowledge that even the bar crowds were happy to listen to original material providing it was good enough, a fillip that encouraged him in his own songwriting.

The Rest were comfortably able to pack out the Jersey locale for show after show and soon were moving in rather more exalted circles. In 1979, while John was still – technically at least – a schoolboy, they opened a show at the Freehold Raceway in New Jersey, third on a bill that comprised Southside Johnny and headliners Hall & Oates. The 20,000 strong crowd gave Bongiovi his first close-up glimpse of the possibilities that rock'n'roll could offer, and he gave a suitably impressive account of himself. Shows such as that were the final confirmation he needed that he had chosen the right career for himself, as he later remarked to *Select*: 'I honestly can't think of anything better than performing in front of thousands of people, all clapping you and paying for the privilege to be there! I would do it for free' – though this last statement might be put down to an over exuberant interview technique.

Gigs such as that at the Raceway had put The Rest on the map and by the beginning of 1980 they had a number of record companies on their trail, Capitol and Columbia going so far as to talk about striking a recording deal. Exposure to the machinations of the record industry was wonderful background material for John; since he wasn't the prime mover in The Rest he could view the situation with a certain detachment, patiently watching it unfold and examining just what it was that a company wanted from a band.

Part of this courtship ritual included the recording of demos, with Billy Squier and Southside Johnny both taking a turn at producing their material. Although John knew Southside reasonably well, he was still a little in awe of the man: 'In those days, Southside Johnny And The Asbury Jukes were The Beatles because they had a tour bus!' Although the demos sparked considerable interest, The Rest never quite reached the tour bus stage; the general consensus was that although the songs were plausible enough, the group lacked the necessary charisma, its focus diluted between mainman Ponti and the young singer Bongiovi. Whatever the case, both Columbia and Capitol passed them by, leading to a little soul-searching among all concerned, the upshot of which was John's ejection from the band. None of the principals have since discussed the reasoning behind this move though it's reasonable to suggest that Ponti laid the blame for their rejection at the door of the singer – the most obvious, if not necessarily accurate, conclusion for him to reach.

21

If this is the case then Ponti was clearly guilty of a major error of judgment and, interestingly, The Rest ground to a halt soon after John's departure. Given his remarkable stage performances later, it's unlikely that John was anything other than a huge asset to The Rest, who were by all accounts a fairly pedestrian rock band. Without a dynamic figurehead, a role which suited John down to the ground, The Rest had little to distinguish them from a hundred bands across the States. Perhaps Ponti was unwilling to share the spotlight. Maybe he was simply struggling to come to terms with the realization that he was not cut out for a life in the limelight and was upset by John's effervescent presence, which reminded him of the missing ingredients in his own make-up. The fact that Ponti, on the demise of The Rest, carved out a career for himself as writer and producer gives added credence to this theory. Anyone who hopes to succeed in that role has to be able to recognize talent when they see it and he'd had plenty of time to weigh up John's attributes.

The unpalatable truth was that by the middle of 1980 John Bongiovi was without a band and had just missed out on a record deal. The future was less than rosy, but once again fate conspired to lend him a hand. Prior to that though, John isolated himself for a spell of hard thinking to ensure that his next move would be the right one. Even if the publicity machine might tell another story, the truth is that John's journey to stardom was the subject of much theorizing, postulating and cogitating. At the tender age of eighteen, John had spent enough time around the fringes of the industry and among established rock musicians to realize that there were certain standards to which he had to aspire as well as certain musical formulas which would provide him with the greatest opportunity of securing a contract. He'd seen how Bruce had formulated his approach, watched Aerosmith, spoken at length with Southside Johnny. As a street-smart kid, he knew the questions to ask and he knew when to listen to advice. With The Rest now a quickly fading memory, it was time to ask himself the hardest questions of all.

If he examined his motivation and determination to make it, he could answer, quite unequivocally, that his desire was as strong as it ever had been and was actually increasing all the time. He could be equally positive and just as honest when he looked at himself as a performer in front of an audience. Naturally there were elements that could be improved still further and there were times when he wasn't entirely in command of an audience the way Jagger or Lynott might have been, but the basics were there. Given further experience, John could feel relatively confident that he would develop the full range of skills required of the very best frontmen. Indeed, by 1980, he could rest assured that concerts were his forte and that people would always be ready to come and watch him. However, he was sufficiently realistic to see that this was only part of the story. If nothing else, his brief contact with the record companies in The Rest had taught him that much.

Since The Rest was put together by another party, John was insulated a little from the personal hurt that Jack Ponti must have felt when his band was rejected by the majors, but he was nevertheless upset by their failure to secure a contract. Quite correctly, but with admirable maturity given his tender years, he took part of that rebuff as being a reflection on himself. Though he wasn't the main focus of the group, he was an integral part of their work and had to accept that, as singer, he might not have put their material across with sufficient skill or vitality. In mitigation he could point to the relative weakness of the songs in comparison with those of a top-class recording band, but he was brave enough to accept that that was only half the story.

Working in the studio with Southside Johnny and Billy Squier had been an eye-opener for the young man who a few months before could only dream of making recordings. It would be harsh to say that John found himself out of his depth in the studio but it was definitely an alien atmosphere to him and he would concede that the unfamiliar surroundings caused a certain discomfort even while he was enjoying the experience. His introversion has already been discussed, so we can presume that his natural reserve was only exacerbated by the pressures that he was under – record companies generally listen for a voice first and songs second. All in all, these were not circumstances conducive to producing a great performance and, from his point of view, the demos were consequently disappointing.

Like all the very best rock performers, John Bongiovi seems to have been born with an intuitive understanding of the medium, an innate feel for what was required. To that he added a sharply analytical mind, enabling him to see clearly where he needed to improve. By the summer of 1980, John fully appreciated that it was in the studio that meaningful, long-term careers were made or broken. So far his experience of the studio had been an unhappy one. Realizing that his apprehension had been born out of uncertainty and an almost total lack of knowledge of the intricacies involved in making a record, he accepted that the only way he would ever feel at home was by spending a lot of time there. And so the next phase of John Bongiovi's game plan was decided on, and this was the point at which fate really rolled its sleeves up and got to work.

3

THE POWER STATION

As he approached his eighteenth summer, John saw many of his friends enrolling in college in the hope of gaining a degree and then a good, steady job. John himself viewed this with disdain. His experience of playing college dances with the Atlantic City Expressway left him with the impression that college life was about little more than getting drunk on a Friday night and, as he freely admitted, 'I already knew how to do that.' Realistically, John had never seriously toyed with the idea of further education, his mind absorbed for the past half-dozen years with dreams of a musical career: 'I knew there was nothing else in my life but this. Don't bore me ... I will be making records. My only concerns were eating dinner, playing a bar and how was I gonna convince guys to play originals.' With that at the forefront of his mind, he'd been undergoing his own kind of educational programme in Asbury Park, learning at the feet of Bruce and Aerosmith. Now that his time with The Rest was at an end, he knew it was the right moment to move on and, following his carefully constructed plan, he began to look for studio experience.

John was indeed fortunate that music ran in the family for his second cousin, Tony Bongiovi, was a highly successful engineer and producer who co-owned and ran the Power Station in New York, one of America's finest and most respected recording studios. The studios were enjoying a particularly purple patch which extended from the late seventies into the early eighties, when Chic's Nile

Rodgers and Bernard Edwards were patenting their disco groove, drawing in many other musicians such as David Bowie and the Rolling Stones who were looking to catch some of their magic. Tony had seen his cousin with The Rest and was apparently impressed with the potential displayed by this distant relative. Now Rest-less, John met up with Tony and explained his ideas for the future, impressing him with his clear-eyed determination and thoroughly professional attitude.

As a consequence, Tony decided to offer John a job working in the Power Station, essentially as a gofer, though this is a little demeaning since Tony viewed him as a potential recording artist and viewed his appointment as an investment in the future. For John this was exactly the breakthrough he required. Although there was no technical element to his job – he wouldn't even be progressing to the relatively lowly post of tape operator – it provided the perfect opportunity to observe the workings of a state-of-the-art facility. The downside of it all was the pay: he earned $52.50 per week at the start of his two-year stay there. The exposure to the record industry though was priceless, as he later informed *Sounds*: 'It's where I got my apprenticeship with the whole CBS/Epic record company, the vice-president used to talk to me like I was his grandson . . . He wasn't interested enough to sign me, but he was like a father figure, teaching me the ropes. It was a great learning experience.'

Keen to capitalize on this golden opportunity, John put his – admittedly mild – drug experiments of the past firmly behind him and went to work with a will, as he told the *NME*: 'I did drugs, but it didn't work out for me. I flipped out, I couldn't handle it.' He did know how to handle a broom though and over the next two years he went through the list of menial jobs from making coffee to running errands. While this was going on he was soaking up the information he needed so that when his turn came he could grab the chance with both hands. Even so those two years were sometimes less than idyllic, as lack of money meant he actually lived at the studio: 'I slept on a pull-out couch . . . [Tony] let me stay there.'

Again his introspection made life harder for him away from

music. When there were songs being played, rehearsals or takes being run through, John came alive and could hold his own with anyone. But away from the music he stayed a loner, recalling in *Q* that 'Not knowing anybody in town, there'd be lots of nights going to movies by myself'. This reflection on his detachment from any kind of social life gives a strong hint as to why he set up a group later on, rather than carrying on as a solo performer in his own right. John missed the company of like minds who were as fiercely committed to the task in hand as he was; he could talk for hours with close confidants but would revert to shy type with outsiders. Creating his own band would give him a degree of security that a solo performer might miss.

John assimilated studio craft at an alarming pace, happily filling that particular gap in his knowledge. Watching the likes of Keith Richards, Brian May, Freddie Mercury or Mick Jagger using the studio as just another tool of the trade was both inspirational and reassuring; any residual fears he might have had of recording were quickly banished from his mind. To observe these rock legends whom he had grown up admiring at such close quarters was an eye-opener, but it wasn't only their musicianship and creative talent that made an impression on young John: 'They were all really nice to me. It generally went the bigger the star the nicer the person.' This was another lesson quickly digested, for despite his success he has retained a healthy reputation for being very approachable.

The next step was to put his new-found studiocraft into operation, though one attempt wasn't quite what he had intended; for a Tony Bongiovi-produced novelty album on the theme of *Star Wars* at Christmas, he sang on a track which rejoiced in the title 'R2D2 I Wish You A Merry Christmas'. There were greater glories to come however. Utilizing the down time that appeared at the oddest of hours when there was no-one else working at the Power Station, he began to put his own songs on tape, for songwriting had been one of the ways in which he'd whiled away the lonely hours. Initially, he worked alone on this material, turning his hand to whatever instruments were available or calling on anyone that might still be around the Power Station, but he quickly became dissatisfied with this arrangement which offended his professional sensibilities. With a backlog of material on his hands, he and Tony managed to rope in an assortment of friends and acquaintances to help out in a pick-up band called The Lechers. It was made crystal clear that these were merely backing musicians organized to help the singer on to greater glories and the camaraderie that John was hoping for didn't really materialize, understandably enough given that the others were just hired hands. Equally inevitable for a group with no real ties, the line-up constantly fluctuated, but at least they did play local clubs in and around Manhattan, allowing John to maintain his on-stage prowess and develop this in parallel with his songwriting and recording talents.

As an onlooker on the periphery of the rock scene, John continued to scheme and plan for his future. There were times when he was racked with doubt, wondering if his dreams would ever come to fruition, as he admitted in *Q*: 'It was tough not knowing what your future was, for a few years there. But you live to tell.' That last sentence indicates the indomitable nature of his spirit and the fierce determination which had already brought him further than many hopeful rock'n'rollers ever reached. It was this that pulled him through the dark times until he could again allow that he was in a privileged position. The arrival of someone like David Bowie at the studio would quickly remind him of his goals and he would be raring to go.

A few moments of doubt aside, John Bongiovi appears to have been totally convinced that he was going to make it, that one day he would prowl the same stadiums that Queen or The Rolling Stones had dominated. Rarely does he seem to have considered failure: he *would* one day occupy the same sphere of influence as his heroes. Encouragement came from those he looked up to, as one story he recounted for *Q* illustrated.

I was getting out of a cab, we were scraping our money together to pay the cab fare ... John Lennon had just been shot and I'm paying off the cab driver and I looked up and just suddenly saw this flash! flash! flash! Then I saw Mick Jagger and a couple of guys standing there looking pretty stunned because this photographer had just jumped out of this garbage can ... Mick obviously knew this photographer but he still didn't want his picture taken but the photographer was still going 'Mick, please let me have a picture of the Stones' so Mick put his arms around me and my guys and said 'This is the new Rolling Stones' and called us the Fabulous Frogs or something and we had our pictures taken with him ... I was blown away.

Moments such as these merely strengthened his resolve to enter the musical firmament.

He was beginning to lose a little patience with floor cleaning and when The Lechers dissolved, he concluded that it was time for him to get serious with a new group, this time called The Wild Ones. Still the chemistry between the musicians didn't gel, which increased John's frustration with his circumstances. Time for further soul-searching and reflection on the previous few years. The best and most successful band he'd been in to date had been The Rest, but they had lacked the necessary ability to progress to recording status. Returning to basics with the requisite studio experience under his belt, he looked at the other requirements for success.

First and foremost, a band needed a focal point which would attract people and put across their message. Beyond that, the group itself needed to be focussed on what it wanted to achieve. John was single-minded in his drive to be the best and so he would have to surround himself with like minds, not the easiest of tasks given that John Bongiovi was not a household name but, to all intents and purposes, just another hustler looking for a break. Observing the Stones and Chic at close quarters, two very different groups, he came to appreciate the difference between competent musicians and those that could be considered professionals. Though they worked in diverse fields, Edwards, Rodgers and drummer Tony Thompson from Chic were, at the very least, the musical equals of Bill Wyman, Keith Richards and Charlie Watts. Both camps were in hugely successful bands at the top of their stylistic tree. Seeing them working made it clear to John how much groundwork had been laid in reaching that standard. It was this that caused him to contact

David Rashbaum once more. Tiring of classical training, David was only too happy to link up with his old friend again and play some of the music that he loved the most. David's return was the signal that John was taking musical proficiency very seriously indeed.

In more downbeat moments, John must have wondered whether it was mere chance that such an ideal blend of personalities such as those that made up the Stones should happen upon one another, but again his tenacity of vision carried him through. He'd seen the camaraderie of the Jersey streets where he'd grown up, it was just a question of careful selection of the right people.

A degree of musicianship and a streak of individuality duly classified as central ingredients of a successful band, John cast around for further inspiration. Image was obviously important, particularly as the eighties progressed and the video revolution was starting to play an increasingly significant role in the promotion of new artists. Well aware of his own good looks and charismatic charm as singer and frontman, John would have understood the importance of a band's presentation and would have had to add that particular element to the mix, though this was something that would have to come together once a stable line-up had been finalized.

It says a great deal about the values of the 1980s that the last subject we address is the songs themselves, since they had been relegated to their lowest level in popular music history. Any aspiring writer had to come to terms with the fact that most bands were trying to write their own songs and so competition was bound to be fierce. When you then considered that most companies had dedicated songwriters on their books through their publishing arms, you could pretty soon have a flourishing inferiority complex. As a long-standing music follower, John was a songs man rather than one who liked to hear self-serving musical doodling, and at a time when so many hotshot players were falling into the trap of constant soloing to the detriment of a song, this was an important advantage. Over his two years at the Power Station he honed his songs, prized economy above all else and drove himself hard to create serviceable hooklines that would catch the ear of a producer, an A&R man or a radio programmer. He recognized that he was setting himself a Herculean task in beating off established writers, but his approach was sound and the groundwork excellent.

If you had any songwriting aspirations and were keen to learn your craft in order to acquire a natural feeling for what worked and what didn't, there were few better places to learn than the Power Station in the early eighties. Quite literally, the place was a hit factory with chart-topping records apparently coming out of its sacred portals every other day. It was a stroke of fortune to which John readily admitted, suggesting that the studio's sublime pop sensibility was at the very root of his early commerciality. Speaking to *Sounds* on the release of the debut album in 1984, he argued that 'our music leans towards more melodic rock because I had that upbringing within the industry as opposed to sitting in my room listening to Led Zeppelin records'.

John's songwriting had been coming along in leaps and bounds, inevitable perhaps given the exalted company he was now keeping – some of their talents had to rub off on him. By the middle of 1982, he had a song called 'Runaway' which Tony Bongiovi reckoned had hit potential. This time the demos weren't going to be recorded by uninterested hacks but by seasoned session players who Tony knew and trusted. Most impressive of all perhaps was the recruitment of Roy Bittan to play keyboards; Bittan was a member of Springsteen's legendary E Street Band and his presence gave an extra stamp of authority and authenticity to the proceedings. 'Runaway' caught John at the end of a lengthy learning process, finally putting all the wisdom he had accumulated into practice.

From this distance, 'Runaway' sounds like a well-arranged run-through of hard rock clichés, the lyric centred on the perennial theme of bad girls and escapist dreams, the harmonies owing something to Queen most particularly while the early guitar pyrotechnics also nod in the direction of Brian May. 'Runaway' is more significant in terms of what it hints towards rather than what it actually delivers. As a concise example of hard-edged pop, it's easy on the ear but scarcely memorable. What does make an impression is the strength of John's voice and the intensity of his delivery. It's often said that once you can fake sincerity you've got it made, and the hard rock/heavy metal genre certainly has its fair share of chest-beating con-men, but the desperation in Bongiovi's voice was tangible, betraying the increasing concern with which he viewed his future.

If it hasn't survived the test of time as well as other songs he's written, 'Runaway' did seem to be right for 1982. For fans of melodic hard rock, these were dark times. On the one hand there remained the hoary old heavy metal bands and a newer crop with an even more extreme sound in the wake of Motorhead, while on the other, softer rock had reached criminally bland proportions with the advent of bands such as Saga. There was clearly a niche in the market, for an artist such as John would add a bit of a bite to the softer end, attracting devotees from both camps as well as those who preferred the middle ground.

With his confidence increased on hearing the impressive results of the demo session, John was set to execute the last and most important phase of his plan, gaining record company interest and then turning that into a contract. By now a seasoned observer of record company politicking, John was shrewd enough to grasp that once one company became interested in an act, many of the others would suddenly pay equal attention to this new artist in case they were missing out on something – doing your A&R based on blind panic was every bit as popular as actually putting in the proper legwork.

With the record industry mainly operating out of the west coast, Los Angeles in particular, John needed to make a decision as to his next move. That was eased considerably when 'Runaway' and three other songs were shipped out to all the east coast labels under the moniker Johnny B., causing nary a flicker of excitement – though in fairness that ponderous pun on 'Johnny B. Goode' was nauseating enough to turn anyone's stomach before playing the tape. Leaving the Power Station behind, temporarily at least, he and David Rashbaum travelled to LA. This showed a commendable faith in his own ability and in the commercial viability of the 'Runaway' demo which he used as his calling card. Holed up at the A1 motel, the pair wore out their shoe leather in visiting literally every record company to extol the virtues of John's demo and musical prowess.

Though he had studied all the angles, he couldn't cover all the bases. In the final analysis, whether he got a deal or not was down to record company tastes. The Wild Ones were neither one thing nor the other; neither heavy metal nor soft rock sophisticates, they were a band out of time. John may have realized this a little earlier – sending 'Runaway' out under the Johnny B. heading rather than billing it as The Wild Ones was a tacit acceptance that perhaps they were not the future of rock'n'roll after all.

At the end of his sojourn in Los Angeles, John had to return to the drawing board. He retained his unswerving faith in both himself and his songwriting but had to accept that at present the other elements that he had considered weren't quite in place. He'd striven hard to plug all the gaps but was forced to concede that the absence of a strong group identity was a stumbling block. Without that potent image, record companies would be worried about finding a commercial hook to hang them on and market them from. Understandably, John was downcast and even humiliated at his west coast failure and returned home with renewed doubts as to whether or not he would ever lay his hands on the grail – a contract with a major label. Yet he was closer than he knew, for without realizing that anything untoward was happening, thanks to the freakish nature of the music industry he was on the verge of a hit single.

4

RUNAWAY

A number of very radical groups have emerged from America with, in the last decade, bands such as R.E.M., Jane's Addiction, Nirvana, Black Flag and Husker Du producing music that has helped revitalize the European scene. However, the vast majority of its most economically successful artists have rarely pushed back musical boundaries to any real extent. As a product of the Power Station, John knew the kind of hard work and attention to detail that went into the production of a radio-friendly tune. His songwriting had progressed to the point at which Gary U.S. Bonds recorded John's 'Don't Leave Me Tonight' on Springsteen's recommendation. It was all the more surprising then that the record industry was unwilling – at the very least – to finance further demos, even if they didn't immediately go the whole way and sign him up to their roster.

With a nifty piece of lateral thinking, John, in the company of Power Station staffer Ray Willhard, concluded that if the record companies couldn't recognize a hit song, the radio stations might. The Johnny B. 'Runaway' track was sent out to WAPP, a new radio station on Long Island that was trading in the classic rock format, featuring the likes of Led Zeppelin, Thin Lizzy, Aerosmith, AC/DC, Rush and so on. The station had organised a 'Rock to Riches' competition, open to new bands in the area who were still looking for a deal. The programmers were instantly struck by the commercial nature of 'Runaway' and began to promote it.

The greatest stroke of luck came when they chose to include it on a compilation album of the event. WAPP was owned by Doubleday, one of America's biggest multi-media corporations. As part of their operation they owned a host of radio stations nationwide, all of whom were issued with this new compilation record. John's 'Runaway' was by far the most commercial offering, and by the start of 1983 it was being aired across the country, achieving minor hit status. John was now experiencing the final few months of normal life – for after 'Runaway' things would never be the same again.

The sudden success of 'Runaway' couldn't have come at a more opportune moment for Bongiovi who, in the pursuit of a record deal, had been running up substantial debts. By his own admission, 'I walked into my first record three, four hundred thousand dollars in debt. Couldn't pay a band, couldn't do anything.' There's nothing so good at sharpening the mind and the instinct for survival as enormous debt and this was a factor that had a large part to play in his development as a writer. With neither the time nor the inclination to produce left-field music, John's financial plight only served to push him further down the road of shameless commercialism. He admitted in *Sounds* that he wanted to 'write three and a half minute songs. I know that the hook has to be there for it to be played on the radio, to sell records, so we can make enough money to make more records.'

Some would regard this as a terrible confession of compromise and sell-out, but those claims need to be tempered with a dose of realism and an understanding of John's musical background. The music that had inspired him had always been good time rock'n'roll; he was not ashamed of liking Aerosmith or The Rolling Stones but wore their colours as a badge of pride. He had always hoped to follow in their footsteps and those of Springsteen and Thin Lizzy and was willing to do whatever was necessary to make the dream come true. His songwriting was naturally commercial and was derived from the classic rock genre that he had loved for almost a decade. This was his kind of music and he made no apologies for it. He would have to concede that he trimmed some of his musical excesses, worked on a song's weaknesses and arranged the songs with careful deliberation to ensure that his strongest suit, melodious hooklines, shone through and caught the ear of the casual listener. That approach is one of consummate craftsmanship rather than compromise. Had he been an avant-garde jazzer who switched to songs like 'Runaway' for financial gain, that would have been an appalling confession of failure and an artistic betrayal, but 'Runaway' was the natural sound of John Bongiovi's music. If you didn't like it, that was fair enough, but at least it was presented with commendable honesty.

With 'Runaway' attracting so much attention, John was now besieged by the very companies who had discarded him just a few months earlier. As things progressed, it eventually boiled down to a straight fight between Atlantic Records and the Polygram operation for John's valuable signature. This is especially significant: it was John alone that the companies were after for he still had no real group. The reasoning behind that was perfectly rational, John couldn't afford to pay any musicians to work with him on a full-time basis. Ideally in the future he wanted a group comprising a mix of ambitious, up-and-coming players of his own age together with a couple of battle-hardened guys who knew the live circuit well but who were looking to flex their musical muscles in a recording band. His problem on that score was that the cover band circuit was still a lucrative one – prior to joining Bon Jovi, Alec Jon Such was in a group called Phantom's Opera that made '$3,000 a night at weekends'. Anyone stepping outside that protective net would have to accept a substantial cut in wages for the privilege of working with John. Understandably, few were willing to do so, and so the construction of a band was put on the back burner until a contract was finally inked.

With a couple of companies in hot pursuit, John was in the ideal position to edge the asking price higher and higher and was finally able to secure a financially advantageous deal that dispelled his immediate worries. In addition, the level of outlay that Polygram offered indicated that they viewed John as an artist with a successful future ahead of him during which they would more than recoup their investment, rather than seeing him as a one-hit wonder. He wasn't solely interested in monetary considerations, however: 'Atlantic were going around saying "this is our new band!" but I really felt at home with Polygram, there's nothing they won't do for [me].'

The reality was rather different – for Polygram weren't the benign benefactors that John chose to paint them. In fact he was offered a deal by Atlantic; he simply went to Polygram's door and told them to better it. Derek Shulman, their A&R man, finally got John's signature on July 1st 1983. Shulman and John got on well, Shulman having had band experience himself back in the 1970s with prog-rockers Gentle Giant, and was able to pass on tips to Bongiovi. Others at Polygram weren't so accommodating, insisting that John front a band and call them Victory, changing his name to Johnny Lightning. Strenuous arguments ensued before some kind of compromise was achieved, but John was definitely having none of Johnny Lightning.

If you do want to beat John with the stick of unacceptable compromise, then this is the time to do it. He has argued that since 'Runaway' had been a success under the name Johnny B., he wanted to distance himself from that and did not want to be a solo artist either. The latter part of that argument rings true. He *was* keen to feel the camaraderie of a band and shelter within its protective umbrella. The name is another thing entirely. John says that he didn't want to confuse people by calling it Bongiovi. Quite how Bon Jovi is less confusing is anyone's guess. The facts seem to be that Polygram weren't happy with the name Bongiovi, judging it unwieldy and, perhaps, baulking at the Italian connotations; this is backed by the change from John to Jon overnight. Although Jon Bon Jovi has repeatedly stressed that he was happy with the name change, it smacks of record company prejudice and it is at odds with his professed pride in his Italian roots. Those roots, it should be noted, were rarely exposed or discussed until Bon Jovi were a major league band.

Rashbaum – as he still was in 1983 – was the only definite fixture in Jon Bon Jovi's mind for his proposed band. With a contract in his pocket and album sessions planned for the very near future, Jon was suddenly a very much more attractive proposition for local musicians, so much so that he was able to pick and choose the people that he wanted. Rather than call in some of the many sessions players that had passed through the Power Station over the previous couple of years, Jon decided that he would return to his roots and select players from his own background, the Jersey bars.

This was a significant decision bearing in mind that he was looking for a rhythm section in particular. Going back to Jersey made it very clear what kind of music he was looking to produce, a no-nonsense rock'n'roll sound. No time wasters need apply. He'd seen enough groups in this neighbourhood to realise that there was a wealth of untapped talent in those bars. Equally important, those bar bands were filled with characters just like Jon himself, from the same backgrounds with the same taste in music. Without the opportunity to build up a group rapport over a number of years, since the studio was already beckoning, Jon accepted the need to hand pick players who would gel together without any difficulty. In such situations, the maxim of 'stick with what you know' is eminently sensible.

Alec Jon Such, another Perth Amboy alumnus, was the first to be recruited to the fold. Considerably older than Jon and David (he was born on 14 November 1952), Alec provided the experience that Jon was looking for to balance his own youthful exuberance. Again, Polygram questioned Jon's wisdom, and ordered him to get rid of Alec – but this time he stood firm. Alec's ability was never in question so Polygram's objections must have been purely cosmetic, indicating the way in which they were looking to market Bon Jovi in the coming years. With Jon as the obvious pin-up, Polygram were looking for a collection of pretty boys to surround him. Mr Such could be called many things, but 'pretty boy' would not be one of them. Jon was looking for character in his troops though, and Alec fitted the bill remarkably well, his solid bass playing suited to Jon's less frantic rock material. In the end, Polygram had to settle for lying about his age.

A similar problem befell the next man to join Bon Jovi, drummer Tico Torres. Born in Colonia, New Jersey on 7 October 1953, like Such he had earned his stripes in an assortment of bands both live and in the studio. Getting Torres in was Such's suggestion and, intelligently, Jon listened to the advice of the bass player. After all,

Torres and Such were going to have to form the backbone of Bon Jovi's sound so it was as well to get two guys who enjoyed working together and had a musical empathy and respect. Jon's only reservation was that Torres had once replaced Vinny Mad Dog Lopez of his beloved E Street Band in another group, Lord Gunner, and Jon had still not forgiven him! Eyebrows were again raised at Jon's choice of colleague, but after their failure to remove Such no-one was going to try to oust Torres.

Such an image-obsessed attitude has to beg the question 'Were Bon Jovi manufactured?' Insofar as Jon did not have a group to back him and Polygram signed him alone to their label, there's a grain of truth in the idea. Certainly there was no opportunity for any organic evolution that a band like Def Leppard enjoyed. They were a band before they hit the spotlight. Bon Jovi went about things in precisely the opposite fashion. Though not wishing to decry the input of Such, Torres or Rashbaum, everything was geared to capitalize on Jon Bon Jovi. He was the undisputed star of the show: it was his songwriting that had attracted Polygram, his performing style that they felt would wow the fans and turn Bon Jovi into a massive success. From Polygram's point of view, the remaining personnel were a matter of little interest as far as musicianship went. They were simply keen to ensure that his colleagues were young enough and photogenic enough to maintain the marketing strategy that they were planning.

Part of the reason that Polygram had to give Jon his head was that he was the only member of Bon Jovi under contract. The others were his employees; as he was signing the pay-cheque, it was his decision who should join the band. This again is a situation very different from most groups who grow up together and have a street gang mentality. There may be a hierarchy in the group – Phil Lynott was always the master in Thin Lizzy, for instance – but there is still a bond between the individuals for they are all a part of the group, all signed to their label and so on. If the band does well, they all do well – not only financially but in terms of confidence, respect, security and self-esteem. Although groups tend to be volatile entities with a high turnover in personnel – Bon Jovi, ironically, have avoided those pitfalls – there is far more sense of belonging in a democratic unit like U2 than in a band like Bon Jovi. It didn't happen, but on a whim Jon could have simply turned to Tico or Alec and fired them on the spot. In his defence, you could argue that in the early days at least they had greater security than he did. They were getting wages when all Jon was doing was racking up bigger and bigger debts for studio time. If Bon Jovi had failed, Jon would have been left in financial ruin where Alec and the others could have just looked for another session job, Jon having paid them up until the collapse of the band.

The central reason for giving employee status to the others revolves around his self-confessed condition as workaholic, from which it's easy to deduce that he's a control freak too, further evidence supplied by his reluctance to take on a manager, of which more later. While everyone was on wages, Jon would be able to call the shots, keeping order by virtue of the employer/employee demarcation line. The very name Bon Jovi made it apparent that there was a very well defined pecking order within this group and nobody should forget it.

Though Jon Bon Jovi remains a down-to-earth guy there is a very strong streak of arrogance in him. Maybe it's just pride in his achievements – he's certainly entitled to that – but his conversation is peppered with phrases such as 'my audience', 'my band', 'I played Donnington', 'I sold 8 million records', which do not reflect well on his solidarity with the others. There is a bond between them, for they could not have survived their many and various experiences intact without feeling deeply for one another, but it's a bond that's been overplayed through the years.

Jon could also be ruthless even with those close to him. That was brought home very forcibly when it came to selecting a guitarist. Ever since hard rock came into being as a genre distinct from any other, the role of guitar player has been as central as that of singer. Think back to the bands of the early seventies – with Deep Purple, you're as likely to recall Ritchie Blackmore as Ian Gillan; Led Zeppelin were Jimmy Page's band rather than Robert Plant's; there was a very creative, almost violent tension between Joe Perry and Steven Tyler in Aerosmith; Tony Iommi and Ozzy Osbourne were equals in Black Sabbath, while Angus Young was the centrepoint of

AC/DC's show rather than the late Bon Scott and then Brian Johnson. Even in Thin Lizzy, with all of Phil Lynott's electric charm, Brian Robertson and Scott Gorham took their fair share of the limelight. Picking the right quantities is absolutely crucial.

There are no examples that spring to mind of a performer who has reached Jon Bon Jovi's elevated status without a sizeable ego. Though endearingly self-effacing at times in interviews, this urge to show off and win acclaim is very much in evidence on the concert stage and it is the very core of his attraction to many of his legion of fans. It's obvious then that getting the right guitar player left Jon in a quandary. He needed a great musician to flesh out his songs and to appeal to that section of the rock audience who live for instrumental pyrotechnics. At the same time he fully realised that he would be inviting a rival into the camp, one who might usurp his position.

This all suggests that Jon was mean spirited – which is not the case at all. Indeed he has been more generous towards the band as a whole than he need have been throughout their career, often invoking the individuals in interviews as being central to the group's success. It should be recognized though that the choice of guitarist in particular was a thorny issue, demanding a great deal of thought. In fact, the eventual selection of Richie Sambora reflects nothing but credit on Jon as both a man and a talent spotter. However, Richie was not the original guitarist. That honour fell to Dave 'The Snake' Sabo.

Sabo's elevation to the group was not surprising, considering that he was a school friend of Jon's back in New Jersey. Since Jon would be heading the group alongside a guitarist, he needed to feel comfortable in the company of his accomplice and so plumped for a trusted friend. The fact that Sabo was young and shared Jon's good looks was a crucial element too; while he was prepared to have older guys in the 'back-room' roles of bass and drums, Jon took Polygram's attitude on board when it came to the guitarist. He and Jon would be the ones to appear in most photos and publicity material so it was essential that their joint image carried the ethos of the group and portrayed them as an entertaining, attractive and vital young rock band. Sadly for both Jon and Sabo, his guitar playing, though technically excellent, did not dovetail with the material that Jon was writing. Sabo's style was rooted in the heavier end of the spectrum while Jon required a more melodic influence.

In a less than ideal situation, Sabo survived for some little while, since there appeared to be no better alternative on the horizon. Both Alec and Tico were less certain about his tenure, Tico recalling that 'the first time we got together it sounded like shit. You get everyone trying to do their own thing.' They both had their eye on Richie Sambora, from Woodbridge, New Jersey. Close to Jon's age – he was born on July 11, 1959 – he had turned himself into a highly articulate musician able to draw on the legacy of guitar greats such as Jimmy Page while adding an individual air that was all his own. He had played an assortment of sessions and had also played with the progressive band Mercy, who were on the Swan Song label which was owned by Led Zeppelin. Like Jon, Richie had been something of a nearly man, good ideas not quite coming to fruition.

In 1983, as guitarist in The Message who were backing Joe Cocker on an American tour, he gained a valuable insight into the backstage operations on a big tour. Sambora, like Such and Torres, had, in the words of the hoary old cliché, paid his dues and he knew his own mind. But where the other two were kept in the background, Richie would have to take a much more positive role – for which he was ideally equipped. Needing to find a collaborator, he went to see a Jon Bon Jovi showcase at Such's invitation and found himself looking into his future. As far as he was concerned, he and Jon were already a team and the band was just yelling out for him to come in and complete the jigsaw. Although he had been asked to audition for Kiss – still one of America's biggest concert draws – he had no hesitation in throwing in his lot with Jon Bon Jovi.

The problem was that Jon wasn't so sure. He'd heard of Sambora, Alec and Tico had made sure of that, and had been impressed with other reports. Talking later to Q, he remarked that 'Richie was playing in a band that were doing real well on the circuit and I was pretty impressed by his playing and his presence so I asked him to join.' This is somewhat at odds with Richie's recollection – which is that he marched into the dressing room following the showcase and informed Jon that he needed a new guitar player and he was it. Taken aback, Jon was a little cool towards him at first, backing off in order to show just who was the boss in this outfit. Leaving Sambora to stew for a week, he was then summoned to a rehearsal. According to Richie's version, by the time Jon arrived late for the rehearsal, he and the rest of the band were already a tight unit, leaving Jon no choice but to hire him. This sounds perfectly plausible but for the fact that it's generally Richie who's late and Jon who puts in the hours at the rehearsal studio, but then rock'n'roll is all about attractive myths and trying to debunk this one serves no purpose.

Showing that relentless logic that he had consistently applied to his singing career, Jon had no compunction in sacking his erstwhile colleague Sabo. Once again this exposes the paradox in Jon's behaviour. Professing to be fiercely proud of the 'brotherhood' ideal that ties him to his friends and family, those ties are not sufficient to prevent him disregarding the oath of loyalty if it suits his purpose or career to do so. In the light of their subsequent world-wide fame and fortune, it's blindingly obvious that replacing Sabo with Sambora was the correct decision from a musical and professional standpoint. The consequence of that change was the birth of a powerful writing combination and a notable improvement in the group performance. That, above all other considerations, was what mattered to Jon and he openly admits that his focus on the task in hand is such that 'it causes you to be a little one-dimensional at times'. It's easy to castigate him for looking after number one – though who would choose to behave differently? – but in the light of the great emphasis he places on loyalty, the extent to which he abides by that ideal is noteworthy. It is not without significance that Jon was instrumental in the highly successful launch of Sabo's next band, Skid Row.

The recruitment of Richie Sambora was crucial to the group's future, providing Jon with an artistic partner that he could treat as an equal – though still an employee – and off whom he could bounce ideas. It also indicated the way in which his self-confidence was increasing by the day. Sambora was an assured musician of the highest calibre, had a relaxed charm to go with his undisputed talent and was something of a ladies' man. There was little question that not only would Richie be breathing down Jon's neck as a writer and as a musician but that he would also be highly attractive to the female contingent in the potential audience. The band might carry his name and be focussed on Jon, but Richie could easily have proved to be the more saleable commodity. By now though, Jon Bon Jovi was so at ease with his situation that he had few reservations; he was number one in this Jersey syndicate and he intended to maintain that primacy.

Jon had chosen his musicians with imagination and flair, taking the greatest care to mix and match creatively combustible but socially harmonious personalities. The 'Joisey' attitude stood them in good stead for they hit the road with a vengeance. As their own private army taking their music across America, strong and lasting friendships were forged in the heat of battle, bonds that would endure through a decade and more of intense work. Even now, Jon looks back on those days with fondness, tempered by the memory of the back-breaking schedule. Happy to see the back of cheap motels, bad food and too many shows at a stretch, he concedes that his best memories came when the group was starting out, fighting to get some recognition for their work, all five men united in a gang mentality. It is that 'us against the world' attitude that carries a group through all the hardships it has to endure in its earliest days.

Those early days certainly were hard going. Despite playing regularly, they didn't lay their hands on a tour bus until 1984, as Jon told *Select*:

> We got our first tour bus in January '84 and we rode on it to a gig in our hometown! We got in it at 4 o'clock in the afternoon, hung out there until midnight when we went onstage and then jumped back on it straight after. Hey, sitting on a tour bus in the Holiday Inn parking lot ... I'd made it! I was Mick Jagger that night!

It's anecdotes such as this, told without any affectation, that endear Jon to his audience who revel in his capacity to remain in awe of certain rock'n'roll milestones or performers. The years at the top haven't caused him to become blasé – and his audience appreciate that.

The tour bus made life easier, but more important than playing concerts was the task of recording their debut album, due for American release in the first weeks of 1984. The limited amount of live work they'd done meant that though they had been able to build up some kind of understanding with one another they were still comparative strangers – and the material reflected that.

The debut record went under the working title *Tough Talk*, though by release date they had changed that to simply *Bon Jovi*, unimaginative but definitive. As you would expect, they recorded at the Power Station under the auspices of Tony Bongiovi and his partner Lance Quinn, with Scott Litt – later to find fame producing R.E.M. and Nirvana – sharing the engineering duties. Despite this collection of talents, it has to be admitted that *Bon Jovi* was a less than sparkling debut. Like many relatively inexperienced bands before them, Bon Jovi were still a derivative unit. In rehearsal, they would naturally fall back on influences from their collective past – but such was the limited timescale within which they had to complete the record, they were still at the stage of wearing influences rather than absorbing them and drawing on them. Hints of Queen, Def Leppard, Kiss, Aerosmith and Thin Lizzy were liberally sprinkled throughout the songs, and though there was a genuine level of excitement and energy about the album, it did little more than run through a directory of hard rock clichés.

This was disappointing, to say the least, for it was apparent that Bon Jovi were a band with a great deal of potential and a certain star quality about them. 'Burning For Love' for instance was a typically fast-paced rocker which featured Sambora's guitar playing to good effect, but it was scarcely unique and could have found a home on any number of rock records of the time.

There were plus points to be taken from the album. The songwriting team of Jon and Richie was promising, and maturing. The two worked well together, Jon's tales of love gone wrong toughened up by Richie's instrumental ability. Considering that Bon Jovi had been together for around six months, the album was probably the best they could have done – for musically they were extremely solid. Such and Torres formed a dependable and occasionally inventive rhythm section that rooted the music firmly within hard rock, providing a safety net that allowed Sambora freedom of expression. If there was a weakness it was that David Rashbaum's keyboards were severely underemployed, relegated to providing a few rather weedy synthesizer lines.

As expected though, Jon was the album's fulcrum, everything revolving around him and his voice. Although lacking the control that he showed on later records, the passion and commitment to his task was overwhelming. The voice was strong and melodic, though he concentrated more on the histrionics so typical of the heavier end of the spectrum. Nevertheless, he delivered the relatively thin material with guts and conviction, staking his claim to a musical future. Every line carried its own emphasis, the collection bearing the indefinable stamp of one who instinctively knew that his time had come. After years of laying the foundations, Jon would not let this opportunity slip away.

Virtually every song was sheathed in production techniques, swathed in echo as they strove for an epic quality, but achieved only superficiality rather than substance. This was a necessary evil for Quinn and Bongiovi, since the source material was rarely strong enough to stand on its own merits however whole-hearted and proficient the performance. Written under pressure, the songs betrayed the unseemly haste with which they were composed. 'Runaway' still sounded good and was destined for a lot more radio play, but this was the only real ace in the pack. Perhaps the only other track to disturb the relatively bland sheen of *Bon Jovi* was 'Shot Through The Heart', introduced by atmospheric guitar work before transforming itself into a pleasant enough example of metallic power pop. But these were isolated vignettes.

The album was characterized by an absence of ambition. Richie seemed content to draw on Rush's Alex Lifeson for inspiration, the opening passage of both 'Get Ready' and the staccato riffing of 'Roulette' reminiscent of his style. 'Come Back' sounded like Survivor and 'Breakout' was little more than a doodle which they hoped Richie might salvage with some raucous, breakneck soloing. He could not.

However, this consistent hard rock assault may well have been a very deliberate policy aimed at introducing themselves to a particular section of the market. Predictable and clichéd, *Bon Jovi* was the product of agile minds who had carefully studied the prevailing musical climate.

Hard rock and its heavy metal offspring had long been one of the most successful musical formats in America, the world's key market. In the early seventies it had been the preserve of Deep Purple, Led Zeppelin and Black Sabbath, but by 1983 these were either long gone or shambling shadows of their former selves, replaced by The Scorpions, Judas Priest and AC/DC. The mid 1970s had seen a growth in glam-metal in the shape of Alice Cooper and, most notably, Kiss, while the flamboyant Dave Lee Roth enabled Van Halen to claim an affiliation to the movement. They had toned down the sound from heavy metal to hard rock, the difference being a reduction in emphasis on crunching guitars and greater attention paid to songwriting and melody.

Few would doubt that Kiss rode to enormous American success on the back of their live show more than their music, but they were adept songwriters too, introducing a different element to their audience which has since become a staple for any rock band with an eye on its bank balance: the mega-ballad. With songs like 'Beth' which gave them their first American Top Ten single in 1976, Kiss changed the face of hard rock and have been followed by groups like Extreme – 'More Than Words' was atypical of their approach but a huge international hit – and Poison who had a number one with 'Every Rose Has Its Thorn' in 1988.

The advent of Def Leppard marked the end of the musical rift between the US and Britain as far as hard rock goes, grafting the American fascination with showmanship, good looks and glamour on to British musical values. Def Leppard rejected that age old and outdated view of the rock show and, over the course of their American odyssey, turned them into pleasurable events.

Def Leppard's concentration on the US market was totally vindicated by the success of 'High'n'Dry' in 1981 and 'Pyromania' in 1983. Critics continued to carp at the band and their new musical hybrid, a less caustic concoction which was dismissed as 'lite metal', but they had carved out a niche for themselves.

Determined not to be a five-minute wonder, Bon Jovi, following Def Leppard's example, was happy enough with a gradual build, accumulating fans over time. Musical freedom could follow once the band had a loyal following. *Bon Jovi* had to be written and recorded at speed, and under those limiting conditions it was a natural decision for the band to direct their material into that hard rock camp and its ready made audience, sacrificing their natural desire to expand into other musical areas in the pursuit of wider objectives.

The choice of 'She Don't Know Me', written by Mark Avsec, was a case in point. Generic soft metal on the topic of unrequited love – reprised in 'Love Lies' – it was a Leppardskin clone, embellished with Queen-style harmonies. A serviceable tune that wasn't embarrassed by the material which surrounded it, in some ways it seemed a pointless betrayal of Jon's own talent as a writer. The logic must have been that since the band would naturally appeal to Def Leppard's audience, for the similarities between the two were so striking, they should play up the comparisons and rest assured of healthy initial sales which would allow them to go on to develop a more mature vision for their second record, veering further towards an original Bon Jovi sound. As far as *Sounds*' Jay Williams was concerned though, *Bon Jovi* had fulfilled its brief – 'grab hold of this album if you want a piece of the action' – but there was a caveat: 'There's nothing earth-stoppingly inventive about the type of music being played here.' That was the very reason for its easy acceptance.

With 'Runaway' and 'She Don't Know Me' pencilled in as radio-friendly singles, *Bon Jovi* would alert the world to their arrival and help establish a core audience. There seemed to be no aims beyond getting through to the next record. Safety first was an understandable attitude but it was still disappointing. From Jon's point of view, it was as though the realization of his achievement had drained him, temporarily, of energy, the emotional impact of it overwhelming his creative senses: 'I still have the acetates,' he said, discussing *Bon Jovi* with the naive enthusiasm of a fan in *Q* in 1994. 'I remember getting a box of copies for the family and sitting on a tour bus that night and getting so excited thinking "this is going to be my life, playing bars".' Having achieved his lifelong ambition, Jon was playing things carefully, refusing to jeopardize the future, and it's difficult to criticize him for that. Though he was sure of his own ability, there was a surprising insecurity about him, born out of the knowledge that there were any number of guys in bar bands that could do his job every bit as well. With so much in life down to luck, Jon wanted to minimize the part it played in his future. He'd got the breaks, now was the time to capitalize on them.

The steadfast refusal to take chances was confirmed by the album cover. Rather than any abstract artwork, it featured Jon separated from his band by the archetypal glamorous bad girl of rock folklore. It reinforced every stereotype conceivable – girls split you up from your buddies, girls are sex objects as shown by Jon's lascivious laugh on 'Get Ready', rock is the ultimate macho music and the singer is leader of the pack. Imagery was to play a large part in the promotion of *Bon Jovi* and the promotional cycle was to be equally significant in the evolution of the group. Time to hit the road again.

5

PLEASE DON'T LET ME
BE MISUNDERSTOOD

It's a little odd that a musician who had approached his career as methodically as Jon had yet to engage the services of a manager. Having scrutinized the industry from every conceivable angle, he knew full well the part that managers could play in elevating their artists' profile. By the same token, he would also have been made painfully aware of the way in which many gullible musicians had been shamelessly ripped off in the past by management and record companies alike. Planning a life in the industry, Jon had to accept that in order to survive he would be the centre of a band generating enormous sums of money, possibly running into tens of millions of dollars. All kinds of hustlers would be looking to muscle in on those earnings to extract their percentage – but who could he trust?

He'd already gone through an experience which left him disenchanted with the business end of his affairs – and that was when dealing with a member of his own family. Having taken Jon under his wing at the Power Station, Tony Bongiovi felt that he had expended a lot of energy, enthusiasm, wisdom and, more important, money in grooming his young second cousin for stardom. Like any investor he was looking for a return on his money in the future. When 'Runaway' arrived and Tony organized its recording, he took this as a cue to protect his investment. He persuaded Jon to sign a publishing contract that cut Tony in for a piece of any future action. Jon later ruefully acknowledged, 'I was twenty. I'd have signed anything.' It took time to extricate himself from the deal but more than anything else he was disappointed that someone so close had, to his mind, attempted to exploit him.

His natural instinct was to tighten his control over the whole Bon Jovi operation, but this was never a realistic option. Jon knew just how complex the Machiavellian machinations of the industry could get and, the Bongiovi deal aside, he was no kid, wet behind the ears and ready for scalping. But he was no great financial or legal brain either. The amount of time that even the most general administration duties would demand meant that self-management was nothing but a pipe dream, though he preserved his independence for as long as he could. Ultimately he had to accept that his main obligation was songwriting, recording and touring and that he needed help to make deals, organize the touring schedule, co-ordinate and supervise Polygram's promotional programme and so on.

Taking on a manager was not a step that he entered into lightly and in many ways it's an act that was wholly out of character. Remember that Bon Jovi was technically him and a group of employees – he was in sole control of the group's destiny and if anyone was unhappy with that, they could close the door on the way out. Jon was the key songwriter, he took the design and style of their concert presentation on himself, he chose the set list etc, etc. In fairness, he'd not done too bad a job so far. He'd got himself a deal with Polygram and had secured a support slot with ZZ Top in late 1983, playing New York's Madison Square Garden, something of a step up from the clubs that this unknown combo had played prior to that. Yet it was this very success that made Jon realize that he was taking too much work on; he was to sport a Superman tattoo on his upper arm, but he was forced to concede that he wasn't superhuman after all. *Bon Jovi* suffered as a result and he knew that the next album couldn't go the same way. A surprise package no longer, people would be expecting much more from Bon Jovi in the future and he grudgingly accepted the need to give his full attention to the music.

This decision is the first real sign of frailty or vulnerability in Jon's career. He had always been defiantly self-sufficient in every respect up to this point, relying only on Richie Sambora to any real extent and that purely within the songwriting partnership. Even then, he was to maintain that 'if I write or co-write songs, they are mine to begin with'. The bottom line was that, however much he resented it, he had to get help to run the organization. There was no shortage of takers as soon as he had signed to Polygram, for industry insiders were quick to pick up on his potential. Prior to the release of *Bon Jovi*, Jon put his faith in Doc McGhee, a 32-year-old from Chicago who had spent his life in and around the music business and who had Mötley Crüe, Pat Travers and James Brown as clients, none of whom were setting the world on fire at the time, though Mötley Crüe were setting fire to their own trousers as part of their Kiss-influenced stage act. It was the first time that Jon had ventured beyond the confines of Jersey to find a partner and there's no doubt he was taking a great risk in throwing in his lot with this maverick, given the number of well-established agencies that were in pursuit of his band.

Jon's rationale was simple. McGhee was only just starting out as a manager and had nothing. Jon was just starting out as a recording artist. He had nothing either. With both men equally hungry for success, they might just make a potent combination, though as he remarked with a degree of circumspection at the time, 'he's gotta be my best friend for me to trust anybody at this time.' Jon knew that he was going to be McGhee's meal ticket. He demanded the same standards of loyalty as from the guys in the band. Providing McGhee did right by him, worked as hard as he did and didn't interfere with the music, the two would get on just fine and get rich together. It was a pairing that was to be turbulent but extremely beneficial for all concerned.

Once Doc was on board, they completed *Bon Jovi* and began to look to the future. There was general agreement that as well as playing their own shows in small clubs and theatres, they should take to the larger arenas supporting established acts, thereby spreading the word to a larger audience and getting some experience in playing the biggest stages which they were looking to conquer in a few years' time.

It was a sensible policy. *Bon Jovi* was warmly received by the population at large and reached number 43 in the Billboard charts, a solid if unspectacular debut. 'Runaway' was released as their debut single and crept into the Top 40, the follow-up, 'She Don't Know Me', peaking at number 48 a few months later. There was something of a following beginning to spring up, some of whom remembered the Johnny B. airplay hit, although most fans were new to the band. It was a good start, but nothing like enough to suggest a headlining tour.

If Bon Jovi had a slice of ill luck, it was in the timing of their debut. They emerged at around the same time as Mötley Crüe and WASP, overblown and frankly ridiculous heavy metal bands who succeeded in whipping the moral majority into a frenzy. Even though Bon Jovi were far more authentically rock'n'roll in attitude and in their performance, the cartoon-like antics of these rivals made them appear banal to a scandal-seeking tabloid press who liked to portray rock bands as horsemen of the apocalypse. Bon Jovi were looked upon as wimps in comparison, particularly given Jon and Richie's classical good looks which contrasted with the grotesque make-up of Blackie Lawless of WASP. It led to a public perception that Bon Jovi were a fake band making bland music and hiding behind a pretty image; WASP were, it was alleged, the future of heavy rock. History has exposed that particular myth of course, but at the time it threatened to do considerable damage to Bon Jovi in their homeland.

As a remedy, they agreed to accept support slots from heavy metal bands such as Judas Priest and The Scorpions. The elan with which Bon Jovi launched into these gigs exposed the weakness of their debut record, indicating that underneath the produced facade there was a raucous rock band struggling to break free. Jon recalled those times with mixed emotions: 'We had to go out to fight against that image thing. We purposely put ourselves up against the heaviest bands on earth to prove that we could stand up to them. We showed everyone that we were a rock'n'roll band, that we meant what we were doing.' It was in these difficult, yet rewarding, circumstances that Jon was convinced of the wisdom of a band set-up. What might have turned into a nightmare – five disparate characters who barely knew one another suddenly thrown together for 24 hours a day – became a source of friendship, warmth and escape. According to popular opinion, they might have been manufactured, but after six months on the road they were solid as a rock, looking after each other, enjoying one another's company and behaving in the typically outlandish manner that virtually every band does when it first goes on the road.

Musically they were improving too, learning how to play alongside one another to capture the best sound. Songwriting continued when time allowed and Jon was happy that they were maturing into the sort of outfit that he'd always wanted to be a part of. The workload that they took on was prodigious, an early example of Doc McGhee's propensity for ensuring that his charges didn't remain idle. In the long term, the plan worked to perfection – Bon Jovi visited every town and made friends all over the country, building up a momentum in the process that was to prove unstoppable. McGhee would point to the success of his idea when questioned as to its wisdom by an increasingly exhausted band, who would then troop off to the next tour, his timeless motto 'work harder' ringing in their ears. Easy to say when you can stay at the office instead of climbing on to another tour bus. Bon Jovi had entered a very long, dark tunnel of touring from which they weren't to escape for the remainder of the decade.

While they were touring with the likes of The Scorpions to toughen up their reputation, they were trying to play down their image, or at least that is how the story goes. Jon was adamant that he did not want to be judged on the basis of his sex appeal but on the strength of his songwriting, an entirely laudable aim. He accepted that the opportunity of using his looks to his advantage was something that Polygram would advise:

> I could definitely do it if I wanted to sell more records. But I refused to do the teenage magazine thing. Look at the first album sleeve. It's a black and white cover and I'm wearing a pair of jeans . . . I have to respect myself as a musician not just a pretty face. I have to respect myself first and earn other people's respect in the business.

Having taken on a punishing and not always rewarding series of support gigs to dispel the pretty boy myth, Jon obviously could not renege on that in interviews. His understanding of the press game was sufficiently acute to avoid falling into that trap. Yet he was not as averse to using his looks to advantage as he liked to claim. That first album cover which he professed to be 'real dull' still featured him in a macho pose; it wasn't black and white but tinted, the colouring carefully used to heighten the structure of his face. To top it off, he was sporting a carefully arranged coiffure of the kind that only rock stars should ever attempt. It may not have been Jon as centrefold but it wasn't the dowdy, impressionistic washout that he liked to pretend.

Jon wasn't the only attraction on the sleeve either. For the girls, the rest of the band had obviously found their way to the celebrity make-over and, if they didn't look entirely comfortable with their new clothes (it was a picture that should haunt Rashbaum for the rest of his life and might provide another explanation as to his change of name), it was just as apparent that they hadn't thrown on the first thing to come to hand, as Jon's protestations suggested. If he wasn't going to push the band too far in image terms until he was sure of their response, he still insisted that they be presentable. He knew the value of the teenage market that had yet to be regularly tapped by rock bands. Meanwhile, for the boys who would make up the majority of the audience for their first offering, there was a young lady who was exposing herself to a pretty severe draught. Yet in the topsy-turvy world of hard rock, this kind of female exploitation was deemed to be perfectly acceptable – 'this ain't no faggot band' as Jon, a beacon of political correctness, eruditely explained.

In comparison with Ratt, Mötley Crüe and so many of the other glam groups that were pouring out of Hollywood at the time, Bon Jovi *were* fairly plain. It would also be incorrect to doubt their commitment to the musical cause, a philosophy which Jon instilled in his comrades right from the off: 'I work so hard I'll physically bleed for the stage and I expect nothing short of that from the band, the crew or anyone involved ... it's the heart that drives me through the set, rock'n'roll is heart, sweat and desire.' From anyone else, that might sound like dumb cliché, yet Jon Bon Jovi so obviously and so passionately believed in his music, his band and in the rock'n'roll idiom that even hardened cynics were forced to take him at face value.

Once they'd witnessed the show, few argued that Jon put his whole life into the brief moments he had on stage. Bon Jovi attacked each show with the same ferocity, night after night, wherever they went. Fans who had come to see the headline band rarely left the venue without some abiding memory of Jon Bon Jovi hurtling around the stage singing as though that was the only thing on earth that mattered. For those 45 minutes, it *was* all that mattered. Needless to say, there were some famous run-ins with headliners who did not enjoy the experience of this new group stealing their thunder and their audience. An early tour with the Scorpions saw them reportedly reduced to a limited light show, no stage effects, poor sound and no soundchecks because they were getting too good a reaction, though as Bon Jovi went on to support them again later in the year, a total of four and a half months working together, you have to take the story with a pinch of salt.

What was indisputable was Jon's determination to make a name for himself and the band at the headliner's expense. 'I was the worst,' he told the *NME*'s Stuart Maconie. 'I was a pain in the ass. I'd fuck with you no end. The main acts hated me. If you said "don't climb that ladder" I'd climb it. If you said "don't go into the crowd", I'd jump in. Me and the guys in Ratt, [another support slot] we didn't get along for jackshit. Fist fights every night.' The agony with Ratt was prolonged still further, into 1985 and the release of Bon Jovi's second album. On the basis of a successful first outing, Ratt had booked an arena tour. They quickly found they were unable to fill them without the support of another exciting new band such as Bon Jovi. Jon was delighted with the exposure this gave his group and was only too keen to emphasise that 'I made Stephen Pearcy [Ratt singer] crazy 'cos he had to keep us on the Ratt tour so long. We needed them but they needed us too.' Considering that Ratt had sold three million copies of their album, Jon had much with which to be satisfied.

Many artists are dissatisfied with their lot when forced to tour as support, but Jon took it in his stride, philosophical about the length of time it might take before Bon Jovi became headline news themselves. Talking to *Sounds* in early 1985, he argued

There's no rush. I'd say it could take five years . . . we'll go headline Japan, do 1500 seaters in Europe then go home and open up again, 45 minutes a night . . . I figure we can play the two hits from last year and two more from this year plus two rock'n'roll songs – that's a pretty cool show. I don't wanna bore anybody!

Jon naturally took encouragement from the success that he was having overseas. Japan in particular had taken to Bon Jovi in a big way, continuing their tradition of acceptance of western rock music, whatever its style. Jon rapidly became a teen idol over there and, away from the prying eyes of American and European journalists, the group seemed happy enough to gain success in Japan on whatever terms were offered, playing up to the sex symbol role.

Shows abroad were something of a release for the group, allowing them to play a mixture of supports and headline shows. In Britain, *Bon Jovi* had done particularly well, topping the rock import charts in the three months between its American and UK releases. This had the effect of depressing sales for the official chart since many fans had already shelled out for American copies, but it still reached 71 and caught the interest of the rock press. The first UK shows were supporting Kiss on their first tour without their trademark make-up. With music in a similarly commercial vein, Bon Jovi made sufficient impact to return in the New Year for their own gigs. For Jon, the difference was marked:

I always said I just wanted to play the arenas, but now I realise why people like Springsteen have said to me "I'll never open a show, I'll only headline". Really I'd rather go play a small hall. I know I've gotta do it, it's 17,000 kids. But when we're headlining for just two or three thousand, I know that they're there for us and you sorta get spoiled by that.

Back home in their main market, Jon was concerned that he should earn the respect of his peers for his musical ability. Grudging admiration had been won for their support act policy for they had acquitted themselves surprisingly well alongside The Scorpions, but it was a long, hard road ahead. 'Our attitude has been tour, tour, tour and earn your keep and meet the fans.' However, all work and no play makes Jon Bon Jovi a dull boy. Revelling in his escape from the world and buying into his dream of becoming a runaway, an outlaw beyond the bounds of normal convention, he and the group minted their own ideology; they were cowboys, always on the road without a place to call home. Dumb games got rid of the boredom of touring for a little while: 'We used a blow torch to write our names on a desk and when people would leave their shoes out in the hallway to get shined, we'd mix them all up and throw the rest out of the window.' Later on, Jon was to recall that there were the usual excesses with drink and drugs on the road, though he strenuously denied having any personal interest in pharmaceutical pastimes. His interests were rather more physical.

Inevitably, stories of his sex life began to filter through to the press, who printed anything and everything, inventing a little extra along the way. Jon was quoted as saying, 'It never surprises me how forward some of the girls are ... besides, sex helps you keep in shape when you are on the road.' Conscientiously pioneering a new kind of aerobic work-out, Jon wasn't ready to release an exercise tape, but he was perfectly willing to prove that the concept of the 'new man' had not permeated New Jersey as yet: 'I once got a couple of girls to bare their breasts when they jumped onstage. After they took their tops off I told my audience "we may not be the best rock'n'roll band in the world but we sure know how to have fun".'

Funnily enough, the wives and girlfriends left at home didn't take too kindly to these stories, though Jon tried to wriggle his way out of the issue: 'They'd read stories of what the boys were supposed to be doing on the road. Many of the stories were so sensationalised it was ridiculous but it eats into the girls.' Fancy that. And obviously Bon Jovi did. Constantly. Should you doubt the veracity of the tabloid stories, Jon said this to Q in 1994: 'We got to enjoy the last hump of wild abandoned fucking and drugs and drinking and tour buses.' Unlikely though it seems, perhaps the tabloids were reporting the facts. Jon seemed to enjoy the tabloid mythology that was building up around him and the group, portraying them as he wanted, wild outlaws who ride into town, steal the women and ride out again. Apparently lacking any kind of conscience over his stud-like behaviour, his only misgivings were that he might be found out by his girlfriend back home. Unfortunately, he tried to play down the stories when things got a little close to home, telling *Sounds*, 'I think this'll be our strongest advantage; not to pretend to be "hey baby, we get laid on the bus every night"'. Who wants to hear that shit any more? This band is just five ordinary guys – they go out drinking, they go to work, they do what real people do.' When one considers that Jon had proudly described his songs as being about 'lust, not love', it would appear that he wanted to hear that self-proclaimed 'shit' and also wanted to live the lifestyle. He'd got the life he'd been striving for and he was going to enjoy it to the full without any thought for the consequences.

It reveals much about the size of Jon Bon Jovi's ego that he felt he could raise hell all over the world, stacking up sexual conquests, and still have a solid relationship to go back to. Admittedly he was feted by Polygram, adored by his audience, drooled over as a sex symbol by teenage girls, pampered by McGhee and told he was the best thing since sliced bread by those for whom he was a source of income – that sort of attention might turn anyone's head; but from an ordinary Joe, Jon suddenly appeared to think he was Superman and that none could resist him or his advances. On a casual basis he was generally right, but his behaviour must have devastated Dorothea waiting for him back home. He argued that 'she doesn't mind me having flirtations, she takes them all in her stride'. Possibly so, but presumably she'd rather she didn't have to. The loyalty of the brotherhood obviously didn't extend to sisters.

Jon had been dating Dorothea Hurley on and off since their days at school together and they remained a couple as Jon went off to tour the world. Dorothea could have been forgiven for feeling a little uneasy as to the consequences, and pretty soon stories such as those above began to filter back to New Jersey. Subjected to a barrage of stories concerning Jon's burgeoning sex-God status, it's little wonder that her resolve to ignore the press began to weaken. Their relationship had already been undermined by the time spent apart and the distances between them, and the flagrant way in which he appeared to flaunt his infidelity was the final straw. Jon explained:

> I went out with her for five years but she couldn't handle me being on the road. So I flew her out on the road with me and she couldn't compete with the guitar. I live for what I do and I don't let anything get in the way of it. If you can accept that, I'll give you the world . . . if a woman ever said she didn't like me always being away on the road she'd have to leave – the band comes first.

In the light of later life, their marriage and subsequent parenthood, it's apparent that Dorothea must have the patience of a saint. It will also become clear that Jon eventually started to grow up and accept responsibility; back in 1984–5 he was still trapped in the bubble of perpetual adolescence that the rock machinery encourages. As the head of a group who made a positive virtue of giving their audience a great night out, only ever claiming that they were a good time band, it was probably inevitable that that attitude would spill over into his private life; with the sexual opportunities that constantly came his way, it's unsurprising that a young man fresh from the rush of a powerful concert performance sometimes gave way to temptation.

In a remorseful moment later on he conceded that he had run 'the stupidity gamut', caught up by the speed of events and indulging the hedonistic side of his personality. Yet as recently as 1990, diplomacy was still an art he hadn't mastered. In London as part of a publicity jaunt for *Blaze of Glory*, he encountered Adrian Deevoy for a *Q* interview, just over a year after marrying Dorothea: 'I can't wait to get along to Tramps, the nightclub, because it is full of the most amazing pussy . . . I'm in London. I'm going to try my best to get drunk tonight, to get laid tonight and steal as much money from my record company as I can.' Items one and three on the agenda seemed reasonable enough, but might not the second have caused some upset back at the ranch? Protesting that he shouldn't be taken seriously, he claimed, 'lots of things we do are tongue in cheek. If you can't make it fun if you're up there pouting and posing for the

cameras then you should get out. That's not what it's about.'
Though he laughed it off at the time and may have been mouthing
off to enhance the outlaw image with which he was increasingly
obsessed, it took several more years and the birth of their daughter
before Jon finally began to act and talk his age.

In fairness, he isn't the only musician in the world whose
relationship has broken down temporarily or completely because of
the demands of touring. The aftermath of this first tour was bloody
all round.

> Everybody sold their souls for the band ... there's been
> divorces and separations, it's been real hard coming home.
> Tico and Alec were both divorced through them spending nine
> months on the road. They lost their wives, their houses,
> everything. They came home and it was like "here's the
> divorce papers".

Wounds like these, even though self-inflicted in no small part,
merely drew this group of outlaws closer together. By the time they
came to record their second album, they had become 'brothers,
closer than brothers', as Jon regularly emphasized. The loss of
Dorothea aside, which hurt far more than he liked to admit, Jon
had everything he'd ever wanted and he didn't want to give any of
it up; that intensity which made him such a magnetic stage
performer carried over into a manic lust for life that enveloped
every activity.

Back home for the briefest of spells, he could reflect on some
highly successful shows that had won fans across America and the
rest of the world. The album had achieved a fairly healthy placing
on the US chart (number 43) and had continued to sell steadily on
the back of their live work. Consolidation was on his mind – to
ensure that Bon Jovi would continue recording into the future. With
their own audience ready and waiting this time, the omens were
good. They had broken into the public's consciousness; now was
the time to exploit their reputation.

In conceiving the new record, Jon and Doc ran through the events
of the previous year to decide where they could strengthen their

performance and commercial viability. The music would be written in the natural course of rehearsal work, but what of the promotional side? In the wake of *Bon Jovi* and its attendant tour, Jon was considerably more secure in his role as musician and band leader. By putting himself in front of people night after night, he felt that he had proved his worth and was being taken seriously as a songwriter and not just a pretty face. At the same time, he couldn't help feeling hard done by when he compared his record sales with those of Ratt; whatever faults *Bon Jovi* may have had, it was a workmanlike rock album that made the most of the group's abilities. Ratt, like Mötley Crüe and many of the other Californian glam-metal groups, were a novelty act, a selection of lavish hairstyles and little musical depth. But Ratt had sold three million albums with *Out Of The Celler*. *Bon Jovi* hadn't even gone gold in America, sales coming to a halt some way short of the 500,000 mark.

With greater musical assurance came the desire to start selling some records by exploiting what some saw as their greatest asset, Jon's looks. He ruefully explained that 'if I hadn't sold myself initially as a musician I'd have felt cheap . . . from a business stand-point I should have played it like that. We would have sold more records.' Although everyone in the group and at Polygram felt that *Bon Jovi* had laid a solid foundation, cracks were beginning to appear in the relationship. In signing Jon, Polygram had invested as much faith in the man as his music. They felt his personality would captivate an audience who might then go in search of his records and enjoy them too. MTV was an obvious market to aim at, yet so far there had been no interest shown in their two atrocious clips. To the company, Jon was being perverse in not trading on his looks. Time has shown that he was right. Teenage sensations are here today, gone tomorrow, as their generation of fans grow up; he wanted a career built on solid ground. Through the intense touring schedule, the still largely male crowd came to respect him for his roguish charm and all-consuming belief in rock'n'roll which they shared as a creed. With a devoted core audience and with a definite persona established that was a fair reflection of the man himself, Jon then felt more comfortable with the paraphernalia of stardom, such as videos and photo shoots.

Having bankrolled *Bon Jovi* and preparing to do the same again, Polygram were becoming more vocal in their demands. If only for reasons of job security, Jon was compelled to play the image game, so he and the others dutifully passed through the barber's chair. The stylist charged with the task of beautifying Alec, David and Tico was John Bongiovi Snr. Richie and Jon also underwent the treatment, but that job was simpler. The result was a band that were denying their identity. Jon and Richie were born to look cool, Alec, David and Tico were born to stand at the back. Few were taken in by the transformation. Much of the blame for the poor showing of the second album, *7800 Degrees Fahrenheit*, was laid at the door of this ill-advised policy decision. In territories beyond America it was less important, since they had not been so relentlessly promoted as ordinary guys; in Europe and Japan, the conviction of their live show rendered all else irrelevant. To the American audience, after the band had made such a virtue of their identification with the kids back home in New Jersey, this dalliance with stylists, make-up and so on was absurd. Richie later conceded that this was an error of judgement that was typical of the whole period, a time of constant pressure and frenetic work.

Jon certainly came to regret it and used it as evidence of what could go wrong if he relinquished too much control. He felt that all the hard work that he had done to establish his credibility as a writer and singer was ruined by this compromise. Looking back a few months later, he vowed not to take his eye off the ball again – for it was a combination of other distractions that had left him unable to concentrate on the job in hand and susceptible to poor advice. The hardest thing to come to terms with had been Dorothea's rejection of him during the touring cycle. Although he'd learned to cope with musical indifference when he'd been touting his demos around, this was the first time such a close personal relationship had gone awry and he admitted that it hit him hard, bruising the performer's large, but fragile, ego.

There were indications of the personal traumas that had beset Jon and the others on the *7800 Degrees Fahrenheit* record, so titled since that is apparently the melting point of rock. Although it did not fare as well as expected, it became their first gold album and reached number 37 in America and number 28 in the UK, indicating perhaps that European audiences had warmed to Bon Jovi rather more quickly than their American counterparts. This may well have been a reflection of the times, since Europe – and the UK in particular – was going through an especially drab period: the recession of the early eighties still gripped the economy, leading to high youth unemployment. The escapist fantasies of Bon Jovi were the ideal way of taking people's minds off their troubles – for a kid on the dole in Stockport, the idea of tearing up America with a girl on each arm and as much booze as you could handle was pretty seductive. Added to that, British pop music was exceptionally lightweight, even for that traditionally trifling medium. The Bon Jovi onslaught made a powerful contrast to Wham! and Culture Club, arch-enemies of the metal fraternity. Whereas back in America Bon Jovi could have been dismissed as just another in a long line of rock bands, in the UK they meant a little more.

Jon was quick to notice the difference in attitude and paid warm tribute to the impact the British fans had made on the group: 'I got to know a lot of kids in England who told me how much it meant to go to a show and to have to save the money for the ticket ... what I wanna tell the kids this year is if I can do it, they can do it.' That evangelical fervour was noticeable on several of the new songs. 'King Of The Mountain', an interesting departure that was constructed around a martial beat, was a blatant anthem of pride in their achievements and encouragement for those in the audience that might be looking to follow in their footsteps. Jon's celebration of the cathartic power of a great gig was, according to your opinion, naively idealistic or touchingly honest. 'King Of The Mountain' and its musical companion, the arhythmic '(I Don't Wanna Fall) To The Fire', were the clearest indications yet of his ethos: a dedication to fighting back against the nine to five, doing whatever you had to do to maintain your dreams, to escape from the establishment. Every time he made a record or played a show the prime motivation was his own enjoyment and then, some way back, his financial security – but like Springsteen he did not want to forget his roots. He remembered the thrill he got as a sixteen-year-old seeing Southside Johnny onstage and walking out of a club on a cloud into a world transformed from the way it had been hours earlier. He was realistic enough to know that that feeling might only endure a couple of hours or days, but that was his job -to turn someone else's world around. He hoped to be to a new generation what Springsteen had been to him, an inspiration that opened up a new world. As he told *Sounds*, 'If there's any message in the current album it's just the idea that anything you want to achieve don't let anybody tell you you can't do it.'

A crowd pleaser by both instinct and inclination, Jon opened the album with 'In And Out Of Love', which simultaneously exposed the best and worst of Jon Bon Jovi. A hard riffing stomp that was designed with the concert hall very clearly in mind, it was a romantic view of a band on the run, ripping up town after town – another expression of his outlaw fixation. Lyrically, it was little short of sexist claptrap, leering laughs and groupie exploitation, presumably intended to be representative of a hard-living touring outfit. What redeemed it was the tongue-in-cheek manner of Jon's delivery which left you liking him in spite of yourself, a very obvious nod in the direction of Thin Lizzy as he admitted in *Hot Press*: 'I often thought "how would Phil [Lynott] handle this?" because he was a modern day outlaw. My heroes were always Thin Lizzy.'

'Tokyo Road' was similarly headstrong and gave Richie the scope to extend himself and his reputation further. It throws another light on his relationship with Jon, for despite Jon's primacy in the group he was not afraid to allow Sambora to be the star of the show from time to time. Apparently the story of a soldier on leave in Japan from the Vietnamese conflict, it is hampered by a stilted, hackneyed opening with Japanese girls singing a fragile melody. Despite the subject matter, it still sounds a little like a guilty postcard from the road, while the cynics had it numbered as a deliberate attempt to boost the band's popularity in the lucrative Japanese market where their star was already in the ascendent.

Other legacies survived from *Bon Jovi* – 'Always Run To You' was a routine rocker about cars and girls and 'Secret Dreams' was another lust-drenched passion play – but there was encouraging evidence that both Jon and the band were beginning to grow beyond the narrow confines they'd set for themselves. Though they dispensed with the services of Tony Bongiovi after his financial run-in with Jon, they retained Lance Quinn as producer and flew out to Philadelphia to record. Growing in confidence and liberated from the shadow of his more experienced second cousin, Jon put a far greater stamp of individuality on the proceedings – a calm assurance which found its way into his richer, more flexible voice. Secure with himself, he was also able to draw more from the rest of the group and each could be pleased with his increased contribution. But it was in the songwriting that the greatest leap had been made. Though the final realization of the ideas was sometimes disappointing, that could be largely attributed to the speed with which they were forced to record in order to honour touring commitments. It should not have disguised the fact that a number of tracks were dramatic steps forward.

To Jon's considerable delight, Bon Jovi were beginning to take off – though the journey hadn't been entirely smooth. Aside from the personal loss, he found himself shedding many of his illusions about the romance of the road and the allure of the touring band: 'Rock'n'roll is not romantic. Ninety per cent of the time it's a lot of hard work but if you believe in something you've got to believe all the time.' It was this hunger that enabled him to put his heart and soul into each concert, a passion that has endured and has become his most compelling feature. Yet the realization that rock stardom wasn't the passport to a life of unbridled ease, fun and luxury altered his perspective on life and on music.

In his early songs, his preoccupation was with escape. Real life didn't impinge on his thinking; his sole target was to get away from that and create his own virtual reality. Though Springsteen would use cars and girls as metaphors for escape, his characters would always find themselves back at the factory gates, looking for work or bringing up the kids. For *7800 Degrees Fahrenheit*, Jon began to come to that same conclusion. There remained songs in which he turned himself and the band into the stuff of myth – 'In And Out Of Love' is the obvious example – but increasingly he began to accept that that was an unattainable dream for many. There's a finite number of times that you can tell your relatively poor audience that your unfettered life of fame and fortune is pretty good. In order not to alienate his fans with his own good fortune, Jon turned in on himself to capture songs of defiance and of broken hearts. On *Bon Jovi*, his songs had been those of the ambitious adolescent. By the time *7800 Degrees Fahrenheit* came out in April 1985, he had had some experience of life and love and chose to put those emotions into his songs. Though not yet the finished article, the album was still the better for it.

The ending of Jon's relationship with Dorothea, and the similar turmoil Alec and Tico were struggling through were reflected in the songs. A caustic savagery was displayed on 'Only Lonely', one of the first Bon Jovi songs that could be considered a real original, Jon's gritty vocal suiting the remorseful lyric. Given an opportunity to step out from behind the macho mask, he was all the more convincing, emoting powerfully in a song that was closer to his heart than previous ones had been. It would be misleading to call him a graceful poet, for his words were sometimes cumbersome and clumsy, yet they revealed depths of character that few had suspected – the beginning of a fundamental shift that was to culminate in the mature work on *Keep The Faith*. The same was true of 'Silent Night', an appealing stab at the mega-ballad and written for Dorothea on the end of their relationship. Touchingly sentimental if lyrically awkward, the mood was eloquently evoked by a highly inventive guitar solo from Sambora.

These were fleeting glimpses of a daring originality that Jon would return to on later albums, but as yet they were isolated shafts of promise. *7800 Degrees Fahrenheit* stands as an ultimately flawed record but one which saw a band that would not remain stuck in a rut, one with horizons far beyond the confines of hard rock. Jon was suitably hyperbolic on its release, saying, 'Now we know where we got hurt and there's a whole different attitude, a more hungry attitude this time. As for the album . . . it makes the first one look like kindergarten!'

If sales didn't live up to expectations, the live following was looking more and more healthy, so much so that they secured a prestigious slot at the 'Monsters of Rock' shindig at Castle Donnington, heavy metal's annual jamboree. Third on the bill behind ZZ Top and Marillion, popular opinion was that Bon Jovi were not dwarfed by this celebrated company and that they cemented their reputation in the UK with a storming set. This was a turning point in many ways, since it gave Jon evidence that the hard rock community had taken them to their hearts and respected them as a rock band. After the unfavourable response to their cosmetic overhaul in America, it was comforting to realize that they were still taken seriously elsewhere. This was their very life-blood after all. In a candid moment, Jon confessed to his own anxieties about the future: 'All I did so far was lay the groundwork, now we're going into round two. The very suggestion that this band might not work out scares the hell outta me.'

This element of insecurity might explain why they spent so much time at the heart of the record industry in 1985. When they weren't on tour, they seemed to be in California. Moths to a flame, Jon and Richie were inexorably drawn towards the Hollywood rock'n'roll scene. Spending so much time on the road with Ratt, they'd heard a great deal about the musical network there and were keen to see it in action for themselves. As ambitious rock stars on their way to fame and fortune, it seemed like the place to be. It was, after all, the centre-piece of the American Dream they had both been pursuing for so long, the dream landscape where nothing is real and reality is whatever you want it to be – providing you can pay for it. The superficial glitz and glamour was alien to Jon in particular, temperamentally unsuited as he was to the place, though the easy-going Sambora was more comfortable. Jon liked a good time sure enough, but Hollywood was a touch too much. Where were the real people, the kind of people who paid to get into his shows? Los Angeles seemed full of clothes and devoid of characters; New Jersey was the opposite and it was an attitude that Jon soon began to miss.

With Dorothea no longer any kind of burden on his conscience, he was able to indulge all his desires: 'I tested the waters, the movie star girlfriend, the big parties but I didn't like it, it wasn't me. I could never move to Hollywood because it is Babylon. There's just too many amazing things there. You could really go crazy there. That's a place where fame could drive you nuts.'

He now dismisses his time in California, but it was a pivotal period in his life and career. The *7800 Degrees Fahrenheit* album and its aftermath are best seen as the bridge between getting the band off the ground any way he could and his becoming a substantial rock artist. Although rock'n'roll is now in its fifth decade, there is still no rule book for new bands to follow; that of course is its appeal. But if there are no rules many conventions have sprung up. During 1984–5, Jon Bon Jovi was falling into line with those customs, slapping on the make-up, puckering up the pout, slithering into the religion-revealing trousers simply because that's how Mötley Crüe had sold millions of albums, it was what Ozzy Osbourne was doing, and Kiss had broken through that way too. All that Jon was doing was exchanging the suit he would have worn if he'd had a job as a bank clerk for the expected trappings of a rock'n'roll star. That wasn't what had attracted him to a career in music originally nor was it an accurate reflection of the songs he was starting to write. Patently he was in a state of confusion. Going to Hollywood was just the most obvious manifestation of that turmoil.

Ironically, it was the Hollywood experience that saved Jon Bon Jovi from himself. Looking at the music scene he had become involved with, the way in which he had changed and the effect his limited success was having on him, he knew it was time to reassess. Pausing for breath was a luxury that he hadn't allowed himself since Bon Jovi had begun in earnest at the end of 1983. Now it was no longer a luxury but a necessity. It had been cool analysis of the facts and the future that had won him a record deal in the first place. Application of those same qualities now helped Jon return to his roots.

'If you believe in your own bullshit it's gonna work against you,' he mused later in *Melody Maker*. Questioned about his expectations of stardom, he was engagingly honest:

Convertibles and Mercedes Benzes and wild parties and reckless abandon. And it can be if you want it to be but it just gets boring ... I had my share of fucking my way through Hollywood. There's nothing wrong with that. I had my share of that and I probably limited it because I could've had some more. But to tell you the truth, I realised that wasn't for me, I'm just not comfortable there.

His parents and friends ensured that Jon remained a Jersey boy at heart and helped him remember where he'd come from. By being completely true to himself for probably the first time since Derek Shulman got his signature, he paved the way for the most incredible year of his young life.

6

WHAT'S WRONG WITH BEING SEXY?

With *7800 Degrees Fahrenheit* a fast receding memory, Bon Jovi took a break to recuperate from the previous tour and do some serious loin-girding preparatory to the next trek around the globe. A few months of rest and recuperation were gratefully accepted by the band who were already discovering that life on the road was not the idealised romantic dream they might have imagined.

Their physical exhaustion aside, they could be satisfied with the progress they had made over the previous couple of years, manoeuvring themselves into a position to take advantage of a booming economy and a musical environment that was looking for crisply played, cleanly produced driving hard rock in order to take full advantage of the new hi-fi hardware that was sweeping the world. As the compact disc made its presence felt, so the classic rock format came out of hiding. As the musical times changed, Bon Jovi were waiting to cash in having laid the foundations. Maybe any one of a dozen groups could have been the band of the times. The point is that Bon Jovi made sure it was them, they were ready when opportunity kicked the door in.

Though they fitted the times like a glove, they were not simply manufactured to fit those tight specifications. Few massively successful groups ever are, for such ideal market conditions only ever become obvious with hindsight. You cannot act on them at the time for once you've identified them and set yourself up to capitalize on them, the atmosphere has changed and there are new criteria to be fulfilled. Although not remotely in the same category as songwriters, recording artists or innovators, Bon Jovi were to 1986 what the Beatles were to the UK in 1963 and the USA in 1964. They were simply the right band in the right place at the right time. Thanks to the capricious whim of serendipity, Jon Bon Jovi woke up one morning to discover he need never worry about anything ever again.

The record that worked the miracle was *Slippery When Wet* which has gone on to achieve world-wide sales of around 17 million copies. When an album achieves that kind of status, as with Michael Jackson's *Thriller* or U2's *The Joshua Tree* for instance, it moves into another dimension altogether. *Slippery When Wet* is no longer just a Bon Jovi album but a social and cultural phenomenon.

Initial analysis has to be on a purely musical footing, for it was on the strength of those values that it first came to prominence. As we've indicated, Jon Bon Jovi has left as little to chance as possible throughout his career. A keen student of rock's history, he was well aware that, in the early days at least, a band's reputation is made on the road. It is there that they capture their most devoted supporters, there that they learn how to play as a group rather than as individuals, there that they strike up a bond that improves the musical chemistry and there that they meet the people that buy the records. Particularly in small clubs and theatres, the venues they played as headliners, live shows bind a group and its fans together with shared experiences, however transient or inconsequential the band may imagine them to be. Fans will reminisce at length about the night the singer jumped into the crowd or the guitarist sang a song or the drummer actually spoke. Jon, as a devotee of gigs himself, totally emphasized with those for whom the minutiae of rock were fascinating. With that in mind, he tried to make each show different, injecting spontaneity that was as welcome from the band's point of view as the crowd's, turning each gig into an event separate from every other night of the tour. As far as *Melody Maker*'s Carol Clerk was concerned, he had achieved his goal. Reviewing the Hammersmith Odeon shows in November 1986, she wrote, 'there's no manifesto, no blueprint, no recognition of any narrow market that must be flattered and pandered to at all times. Bon Jovi are for everyone!'

The strength of Bon Jovi as a live band could not be questioned. They were the premier hard rock act on the circuit and had substantial claims to being the best live band of any kind. Asked how he maintained the breakneck pace, Jon confessed, 'you just keep pushing. Keep on fighting 'till the show's over. It's got to be as good as the last time . . . you push from inside. You think back to the time when you had to save for weeks to go to a concert – it's not just any show to these kids, it's the one show of the year . . . I have to remember that. I have to get my ass out there. Don't matter if I'm tired . . .' – an attitude that many performers might learn from.

Jon's motivation was his belief in the virtues and the importance of simple enjoyment.

> We're all part of it and that's why I like to go down and touch the kids in the front row, just getting together with them . . . I want everybody to have a good time at our shows, I want the kid in the 89th row to say 'I swear to God the singer is looking right in my eyes'.

Such passion was a rare thing as rock went through one of its cooler-than-thou periods; like U2 in a different sphere – only they had wriggled free of the glamourous shackles – Bon Jovi were only concerned with providing great entertainment, not looking cool.

The soul-searching that Jon went through in the post-Hollywood period helped crystalize a new direction for himself and the band. The plan to which he and Doc McGhee were working was simple: conquer the rock audience and earn its respect by proving that they were for real and could play with the heaviest bands. They had now reached that point – the 1985 Donington gig had illustrated that. The next phase was to stretch the music further, taking the band to an audience beyond the confines of the hard rock genre. The reasons were twofold; first it provided the group with a new challenge, maintaining their interest in the group and bringing fresh stimuli to the music. Secondly, the financial rewards were far greater at the pop end of the market and Bon Jovi had never been shy of making money even if that was not their sole – even prime – motivation.

In the terminology of the California therapist, Jon had 'found himself' after he left Los Angeles to think. Clearly he had accepted the rights and wrongs of his past behaviour, both personal and professional, regretting parts of it and enjoying others. That firmly behind him, he now turned his thoughts towards the future. That was readily apparent when he and Dorothea were reconciled prior to the recording of *Slippery When Wet*. If it did not completely signify the end of Jon's wild-man days, it was a signpost in that direction. From here on it would be Richie that would occupy the gossip columns with his relationships with actresses Ally Sheedy, Cher and eventually Heather Locklear, whom he would marry at the end of 1994.

Satisfied that Bon Jovi were a solid band on the way up, Jon faced the crucial next few years with renewed determination. Industry rumblings suggested that their time with Polygram was nearly up, though the company themselves deny this as a scurrilous rumour. It's not hard to understand their reasoning though, if such was the case. While Jon and the band would have realized from the growing success of their live shows that an irresistible momentum was building up behind them, Polygram had only sales graphs to interpret and the sales for the first two records had not been impressive, particularly in the light of the success of Mötley Crüe for instance. What the company did not take into account were the long-term implications. Where the glam acts were simply tapping into a transient fashion, Bon Jovi were heading for rock's heartlands and constructing a close relationship with their fans. Where other singers might indulge in the 'star trip', Jon was generally affable and accommodating with fans, signing autographs, having pictures taken with them and spending time talking with them. Again, U2 are a potent parallel in this regard, for their monumental commercial achievements of the late eighties came on the back of a similar bond with their audience. U2 made their grand gesture that won them the world's approbation at Live Aid. Bon Jovi did much the same, though in front of an American audience at Farm Aid. The effect was comparable, since if America loves it today we all get to see it tomorrow.

The real Jon Bon Jovi was back in town and he felt that it was time to make a definitive Bon Jovi record. The first two offerings had had their moments but in truth they were pretty lame affairs; it was the live show that was carrying them through, and the imbalance demanded correction. Shows live in the memory but memory eventually fades. It is in the quality of records that a long-standing reputation is made and maintained.

If Bon Jovi were the right band for 1986, then the constituent parts that made up Bon Jovi were also reaching a perfect synthesis. Hard work though it was, the tours that they had thrown themselves into had been rewarding. They received warn responses everywhere, which in turn stoked the fires of confidence. As a band, they were tight with absolute faith in one another as they effortlessly scaled one performing peak after another. It was this self-belief and camaraderie that held the group together through trying times. There were many, many complaints about the sheer size of the task they'd set themselves, the time spent travelling and the loss of contact with family and friends. So vociferous were the objections at times that given the lop-sided nature of the group's hierarchy, it was surprising that no-one jumped ship.

Alec, Tico and David stayed in the group, something that was a little surprising to outsiders who felt that Jon might have traded them in for more attractive colleagues – never a real possibility – or that they might grow tired of their subservient status. Richie had every incentive to stay as part of the songwriting partnership but the others were effectively hired hands. The financial aspect was obviously important to them because as Bon Jovi increased in popularity so did their earnings. Having put in several years of hard slog, they were unlikely to drop out just as the rewards began to flow. Even so, given the combustibility of some of the relationships within the group, there were many fractious moments. That they survived was testimony to the friendships in the group more than the financial considerations. There was no doubting the ties that bind, as Springsteen might have put it. With characteristically melodramatic flair, Jon told *Sounds* that 'the band is more than friends, maybe more than brothers. It's the band, it's a higher place than to be brothers with somebody. It's like an unwritten law. It's your whole life.'

All these were ingredients which ensured that Bon Jovi were firing on all cylinders going into the next record. If they were capable of making a really good album, now was the time to prove it. The vital step that Jon took was to reject any kind of external advice. Smarting from the mistakes he'd made the previous year, the way in which he'd compromised according to management and company instruction to increase sales, he resolved that no-one would tell him what to do again; after all, it was to avoid all that that he'd become a musician in the first place. Taking a break for the first time in two and a half years, Jon and Richie allowed themselves the time and space to experiment with their songwriting and to really get to know one another. Prior to this, songs had generally been written in hurried moments on stolen days off. With the stakes now so much higher, they were determined to do themselves justice.

To relieve the pressure, they also agreed that they would stockpile far more songs than could possibly go on the album so that they could then select the very best. To facilitate the songwriting marathon, they concluded that they wouldn't enter the studio until they were satisfied that they had enough material; they had continued to put songs together on the road but they were looking to hone it further and add to the collection. They finally decided that they were ready when they'd written '35 songs, Richie and I. When it came to demoing them, he and I produced about 25 of them in a small studio in Sayreville.' Richie waxed poetic about this sudden explosion of material, telling *Sounds*, 'Jon and I, we became a creative reservoir. Something happened and we just locked in. We sat down and wrote and wrote and wrote.'

Anxious to approach everything afresh, they chose to call in a new producer, Bruce Fairbairn, then best known for his work with Blue Öyster Cult. Although the relationship with Lance Quinn had been an amicable one, Jon felt that he had outgrown it. He felt that there needed to be an injection of new blood in the studio, a fresh approach that would question their standard working practices. Further conversation with fans suggested that he was making the right decision:

Some of the songs from our first two albums never quite hit

home until they were performed live. People would come up to us at concerts and say 'Now I get it'. It took them to see us live to really understand what the band's music was gonna be about. So for this album we knew it was time for a new producer. Bruce was my first choice. He was turning down bands that sell twice as many records as we had in the past.

Calling Fairbairn into the team was an inspired move. The change in the group attitude and approach was immediately apparent on the new record, a slimmed down, sparse sound that allowed the songs to speak for themselves. Where previously the music had been too busy, Fairbairn helped the band identify what did and did not work. Harnessing the strengths of each song, he counselled that they should be highlighted not buried. Sambora and Bryan were required to exercise considerable restraint in their playing, which gave Such and Torres the opportunity to take a more vibrant role in the band. Overall, *Slippery When Wet* packed a powerful rhythmic punch that the first two records had lacked. He made the groove obvious, so that it became the core, funking up the Bon Jovi sound, which in turn made their songs far more palatable to pop radio. Fairbairn's partner in crime was engineer Bob Rock whose mixing skills were second to none. Rock's crisp, clear sound separation was instrumental in winning air-time.

Another of Fairbairn's gifts to the band was the inaccessibility of his studio. He was a Canadian with his operation based in Vancouver, so the band had to move out of New Jersey to work with him. This was the answer to Jon's prayers. He'd become outspokenly critical of the interference that had clouded the recording and promotion of *7800 Degrees Fahrenheit* and clearly blamed that for his Hollywood problems in no small part. He was keen to avoid unwarranted intrusions this time around, and Fairbairn's studio offered the perfect solution. It was with great glee that Jon told Carol Clerk in *Melody Maker*, 'to get to Vancouver [the record company and management] would have had to get in two or three different airplanes.'

Although Jon and Richie had demoed 25 or so songs, they decided to narrow down the field to a more manageable fourteen so that they wouldn't dissipate their energies on recordings that would never see the light of the day. This was all just another facet of the newly-minted professionalism which Jon had always tried to follow, but which had been diluted by the pressure exerted by outside influences that reduced him and the band to a package responsible for shifting units and selling tickets. Though none of the band were classic rebels, their reaction to these strictures had been to throw up their hands and block out the rules. This new back to basics regime, with the band living and working together in Vancouver after a short vacation, lit the fire again and they emerged with their minds very much on the task in hand.

The raw material, Jon and Richie's songs, was the best they'd had yet. Following on from the development shown between *Bon Jovi* and *7800 Degrees Fahrenheit*, one might have expected further improvement, but the change this time was dramatic and exponential. With his early songs, Jon had often dealt in bland clichés, aping the records of those who had gone before. As he admitted himself, 'Before, I was just writing songs from the point of view of a kid in New Jersey who'd just heard about the world. Now I've seen some of the world and I'm writing from a different point of view.' He was no longer forced to live vicariously through other people's songs, passing them on second-hand through his records. He had his own experiences to share with his own audience and they formed the basis of *Slippery When Wet*.

Thanks to his New Jersey origins, he'd already become used to people dragging out the Springsteen comparisons, so much so that he had taken to hiding his home state and simply describing himself as an American. This was fair comment, for Springsteen and Southside Johnny had very little to do with the kind of music he was recording initially. He had deliberately set himself the target of making two hard rock albums, a goal he had achieved using Thin Lizzy, Van Halen and Kiss as the most obvious reference points. This reflected just one side of his musical taste though and he was keen to stretch himself further on this upcoming album; consequently the time was right to draw on the Springsteen legacy.

It would be misleading to imagine Jon Bon Jovi approaching Bruce Springsteen's work like an academic, dissecting it to find just how it was structured and how it worked. Jon had been listening to The Boss for a decade now and absorbed the lessons by osmosis. He knew Bruce's music inside out and was himself starting to experience some of the emotions that Springsteen had articulated. But the most exciting thing about *Slippery When Wet* was that it sounded like definitive Bon Jovi. They had, like all the biggest bands, patented a song that was uniquely their own and yet it still bore trace elements of *Born To Run*, most notably on the single 'Livin' On A Prayer'. It was that song – along with 'You Give Love A Bad Name' – that broke Bon Jovi around the world. This was especially significant since these and 'Without Love' were the first fruits of a new writing triumvirate of Jon, Richie and Desmond Child.

Child was well known in AOR circles, having his own group, Rouge, though he was not really cut out for the rock 'n' roll lifestyle. Like Jon himself, Child was a figure who seemed to be permanently on the brink of success without ever quite stepping over the threshold. Their partnership was to change the lives of both men. Jon describes him as 'the greatest band-aid I've ever met, he's the greatest fixer-upper'. In any songwriting team, especially one so short-lived, it's never easy to tell just who does what from the outside. However, given that Child's involvement with Bon Jovi had been almost exclusively on the singles, it's reasonable to suppose that his contribution came in terms of arrangements, structuring of choruses and so on. It is these elements that had eluded Jon in the past, preventing the band from having any major single success. For the singles market, subtlety of approach is rarely rewarded. Both 'Livin' On A Prayer' and 'You Give Love A Bad Name' bore the hallmarks of chart success; the songs were deconstructed and rebuilt so that you were inexorably drawn on to the musical hook, the chorus dealing the knockout blow. A hit is very often a song that you can sing before it has finished playing for the first time. Whatever the parent genre, great pop music is usually big, dumb and simply irresistible. Both songs fit the bill – though 'dumb' does not mean 'unintelligent'.

Naturally enough, many have used Child's contribution to add a little needle to encounters with Jon, some having the temerity to suggest that without Child's input Bon Jovi would be washed up by now. Not surprisingly, it's an accusation he violently rejects: 'What the fuck do we owe him anything for? He didn't achieve success until he wrote with us. He'd written a few songs with Kiss and Bonnie Tyler and none of them were hits. We get together, the chemistry works and we wrote some great songs.' Viewed rather more calmly, there is a lot of truth in Jon's assertion. Child was good for Bon Jovi and Bon Jovi were good for Child. Each learned something useful from the other and each's career prospered in the aftermath, a good deal all round.

To rationalize it all, the Child collaborations may have been the most obviously commercial material but there were no real weak links in the chain. *Slippery When Wet* caught Jon and Richie quickly evolving into a powerful team; maybe they were still not quite there, so Child stepped in to the breach to help with his specialist knowledge of writing for radio. There's nothing shameful in that; needing help, they went to a good teacher. What should never be forgotten is that Jon and Richie provided the basic songs to begin with. Child's role was to overhaul and simplify, helping them to define what they were best at and in the process to set the boundaries for 'lite metal'. The exposure that Child received, allied to the lessons he learnt from Jon and Richie, turned him into a much sought-after songwriter overnight, so the benefits were indeed mutual.

Whatever your opinion on the extent of Child's influence, there's little question that 'You Give Love A Bad Name' was the record which launched Bon Jovi into the stratosphere. It reached number 14 for their first British hit, but its greatest achievement came at home in America where it topped the Billboard chart. There was never any question that it would be a hit before release for all the ingredients were in place and, as Richie was to argue, virtually anything that Bon Jovi had released at that point would have gone Top Ten, such was the head of steam they'd built up through touring. With expectation levels so high, the release of a commercial masterstroke made the number one slot almost a formality. The audience had grown used to Jon's songs of love and betrayal by then, but this seemed more convincing, that conviction giving it its punch.

The single's fortunes were further enhanced when Bon Jovi finally got to grips with the promotional video. Part of their failure in the past could be laid at the door of their inability to secure a heavy rotation slot on MTV. Frustrating for all concerned in normal circumstances, it was all the more so since the group had deliberately endured the glamourization of their image to help sales. Jon was archetypal MTV fodder, but the clips made for their early singles were so uniformly inept that they were never considered worthy of air time by the all-powerful cable channel. Since MTV's influence in the market place was increasing all the time, this posed serious difficulties for Bon Jovi. Tiring of the whole video circus, they took charge of the situation and insisted that they be filmed in a live setting, capturing the atmosphere of their whole show in just four minutes. This was precisely the right approach – MTV loved it and Bon Jovi charmed a new legion of fans who were excited by their intense, yet good humoured approach to the music.

The sex symbol situation reared its ugly head again, with Jon reverting to 1984's denials, though by now his protests sounded rather hollow. Certainly one photo session gave the lie to it all. Wearing just a pair of shorts and a torn T-shirt which he later discarded, he was pictured in a jacuzzi, presumably to tie in with the *Slippery When Wet* title. These were not the kind of pictures normally associated with a 'serious artist' and they did his claims for credibility incalculable harm – Jon Bon Jovi was just a bimboy once again. Though he instantly regretted this particular session, it was too late: it had overshadowed the quality of the music they had produced and put back his cause by several years.

Commercially though, it was further grist to the promotional mill. With 'You Give Love a Bad Name' a hit, he became the face of the moment, and the record company wasn't slow to exploit the hunky image. *Slippery When Wet* quickly settled in to the first of two stints at number one in America, clocking up a total of fifteen weeks there. The second spell was triggered by the release of a second single, 'Livin' On A Prayer', a song which really did tell you a lot about Jon's teenage tastes. For many it was a new reading of *Born To Run*. The perspective was defiantly blue collar, the lyric a tale of love against the odds and against a backdrop of unemployment.

Comparing 'Livin' On A Prayer' with 'Hardest Part Of The Night' on the previous album provided stark evidence of Jon's new eloquence. Where the earlier song had been ham-fisted and couched in he-man language, 'Livin' On A Prayer' was honest and articulate.

The same was true of the rest of the album. Before it was overtaken by events and became a piece of popular history, *Slippery When Wet* was considered as a collection of songs rather than as a milestone. It boasted a nice selection of moods as the band freed themselves from the grim determination to make aggressive music to reinforce their manly credentials. Richie was as keen as Jon that they should be themselves on this new record. The result was, by rock standards, an eclectic bag. For instance, the obligatory mega-ballad came in the form of 'Never Say Goodbye', a 'set 'em up Joe', three-in-the-morning exercise in self-pity that another Jersey boy, Frank Sinatra, might have convincingly rearranged.

The E Street Band were invoked for Jon's solo composition, 'Wild In The Streets', though he had also been paying attention to Marillion at Donington, for the keyboard opening owed a little to their sound. Although rather a slight piece, it caught Bon Jovi doing what they do best, playing good time rock 'n' roll; David Bryan (née Rashbaum) stole the show with a powerful contribution. It was indicative of Jon's stringent demands on his troops that Bryan came through with such telling work, for Jon had accused him of failing to pull his weight earlier on. He responded well and by the end of the recording sessions he was fully integrated into the band once more.

That speaks volumes for the complex, yet basically harmonious, relationships inside the group. Jon himself was a hard taskmaster, demanding the very highest standards from everyone in the band, insisting that they put as much into the group as he himself did. That might be considered unrealistic given the financial imbalance, but everyone benefited when the records sold, even if some did better than others. More than that though, it demonstrates the strong bond of loyalty that existed; Jon did not sack Bryan outright which, as the band's leader, he was quite at liberty to do. Instead, he simply put Bryan in the picture and allowed him time to channel his energies accordingly. At the same time, when challenged by Jon,

Bryan did not flounce out of the group in a fit of pique and sell his story to the press, as has happened in many another band over the years. Eager to retain his place within the Bon Jovi family, David simply knuckled down to some hard work and regained his spurs. You might attribute that to a simple desire to cling on to his income but the evidence points to a deeper friendship than can be explained by mere money alone.

Oddly, money never seems to have caused any kind of rift in the band. The old adage says that there are no friends in business. Bon Jovi is a business and a well-run one at that, but they are the exception that proves the rule. If things haven't always run entirely smoothly, any disputes have generally been the result of tempers frayed by overwork or quotes taken out of context and distorted by the tabloids. Money has never been a bone of contention, a fact which adds further weight to the claims regarding the 'brotherhood' of the band.

By now there were few who doubted that Bon Jovi's natural habitat was the road. Jon had proved to be a consummate showman, holding audiences rapt to attention – but this didn't happen by pure chance. His keen musical intelligence was constantly looking to produce new material that would work well in the live setting and it was into this category that 'Raise Your Hands' and 'Let It Rock' fell. The former was a powerful stompalong, a rabble rouser par excellence, the latter, which opened the album, a further refinement of 'In and Out Of Love' which had been the clarion call to arms on *7800 Degrees Fahrenheit*.

These songs were good solid material that showed Jon's talents off to advantage, but they were eclipsed by 'Wanted Dead or Alive' which underlined the self-confidence that was endemic in the Bon Jovi camp. An acoustic ballad of sorts, in it Jon successfully employed his cowboy/rock'n'roll analogy for the first time. For some tastes it was all too obvious, but it indicated a man a little more complex than many would like to admit. It also suggested that if Jon professed to love the life he was leading, there were misgivings at the back of his mind, a growing weariness with living life away from home which didn't bode well in view of the touring schedule he was about to undertake.

'Wanted Dead Or Alive' became a highlight of the live show, an opportunity to indulge Jon's penchant for the memorably theatrical – performed with just an acoustic guitar on a secondary stage in the middle of the auditorium, Jon reached his destination by being winched over the heads of the crowd below to their audible amazement and excitement. Vaudevillian it might have been, but it was trickery which was appreciated – Bon Jovi became so staggeringly popular they would have got a full house if they had strolled onstage with a 60-watt lightbulb behind them, but with the wherewithal they now had they were determined to put on a show to remember for the kids who might not see another band all year.

Evidence of Jon's insatiable ego or of a concern for the audience that had put him in his privileged financial position? There is no definitive answer, the most likely being a combination of the two, but you could never accuse him of losing sight of his roots once he had got Hollywood out of his system. Having let fame take him away from the things he held most dear once before, it wouldn't happen again. This contact with the grassroots was exemplified in the method of selecting the album's final track listing. With fourteen songs recorded, they weren't totally certain of running order or even which songs should be left off the finished article. On the sensible basis that the people on the street would actually have to put their hands in their pockets to buy the thing, Jon decided to canvass their opinions, no doubt with one eye on the fact that it would make for a great publicity angle too.

Looking back at the final days of recording in Vancouver, he remembered:

Around the corner from the studio was a pizza parlour and whenever we went there there'd be about fifty kids hanging around outside the place. So on the last day we took them all back to the studio to listen to the songs and they told us what they liked and what they didn't like. It was great. Best thing we ever did! In the end I played it for lots of groups of kids but no executive people, no management people.

This dogged determination to exclude any industry types from the whole recording process suggests a man with a point to prove – which indeed he had. If this was to be his last shot, as some suggested, he wanted to be in control of his own destiny and live or die by his own hand. The success that ensued was vindication of this remorseless tenacity of vision and cleared up a long-standing bone of contention; it is the artist alone whose job it is to make a record. He did concede that Polygram was crucial to his success though, saying 'when I turned the tapes in, the record company people were genuinely excited and proud. Those guys have all worked as hard as we have and everybody's sharing in the success of it. It's that kind of attitude. It's a lot of fun.'

Where Jon's instincts let him down was in the sleeve design, a long-running battle which generated into farce. The original artwork featured a buxom young wench in a soaking wet T-shirt that was bursting at the seams as it strained to contain her feminine charms. Three years on from the Spinal Tap movie and their trials and tribulations with the *Smell The Glove* sleeve, you might have hoped that this kind of crass exploitation was a thing of the past. Sounding worryingly Tufnelesque, Jon tried to convince journalists that they were over-reacting: 'That wasn't sexist at all. It was much better to put a picture of her on the cover than a picture of a guy on the cover know what I mean? You'll never find *that* problem in *this* camp. We're not Frankie Goes to Hollyweird.' Polygram intervened and refused to allow them to go ahead with the sleeve, citing the refusal of major stores to take such an offensive cover which would in turn harm sales. Had Polygram not taken this line, *Slippery When Wet*, in itself a title dripping in innuendo, might never have become a landmark release.

One idea rejected – though it did come out, as it were, in Japan – they had to come up with another suggestion. Racking their brains in a photographer's studio in the early hours of the morning, Jon grabbed hold of a black bin-liner, soaked it in water, scrawled the name on it, had it photographed and they had their solution. As Jon later exclaimed, you could then put your own connotations on the title and make it as innocent or lascivious as you chose. It's just a twist, that fine line between clever and stupid.

However, Polygram weren't happy with a black sleeve. 'How

much more black could it be?' they asked and back came the reply, 'None. None more black.' Concerned that people wouldn't notice the album on record store shelves, Polygram fought hard to change the sleeve again, but this time Bon Jovi got their way. If anything, *Slippery When Wet* proved that as long as the music was good enough, the packaging was an irrelevance. As soon as 'You Give Love A Bad Name' and 'Livin' On A Prayer' were played on the radio, the fans went looking for the parent album and had little trouble finding it.

Slippery When Wet became an honest-to-goodness phenomenon, the result of an incredibly lucky combination of events, external forces and a band hitting its stride at precisely the right moment, catching the mood of the times. People wanted fun, Bon Jovi provided it. They wanted singalongs, Bon Jovi provided them too. When it came to the live show, they wanted something spectacular and Bon Jovi were on hand to provide that. The motto for 1987 across America and Europe was 'if you've got it flaunt it', and Bon Jovi did little else but flaunt their enormous wealth on stages all over the world, buying all the latest hardware to create an unforgettable rock'n'roll experience.

Yet things didn't start out that way. To launch *Slippery When Wet* the band had been booked to do another support slot with .38 Special, a hoary boogie band that were still popular enough to play arenas. Pretty quickly their shows were selling out everywhere as people flocked to see the support group playing at the peak of their powers. Having to play just 45 minutes and with their single already storming the charts, Jon was able to perform with reckless abandon – no need to pace himself for a longer show. These shows merely accentuated the Bon Jovi profile in the tabloids; Jon was elevated to mythic proportions.

It was fortunate that as the band were winning undreamt of fame their feet were kept on the ground by support duties. The humble status helped them remember what they were about and where they'd come from and that all the wealth was simply a very enjoyable adjunct to the main task: making records and playing concerts. Jon was honest in his appraisal of the sudden change in status, telling *Melody Maker*: 'The success we're having now is not

From left to right: David Bryan, Tico Torres, Jon Bon Jovi, Alec Jon Such, Richie Sambora, 1986

Jon Bon Jovi, 1989

The runaway, Jon Bon Jovi, 1984

Some good time rock'n'roll; Jon Bon Jovi, 1987

The hottest band in the world – 7800 degrees fahrenheit to be precise; David Bryan, Tico Torres, Jon Bon Jovi, Alec Jon Such, Richie Sambora, 1985

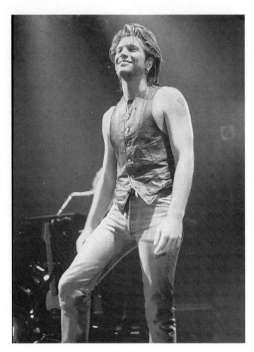

Keep the faith, 1993

as romantic as it is growing up thinking that some day we'll get a record deal ... I don't pay any attention to what we're told about our success. Our attitude is just that we made a record.'

Life was soon to change though as, the support shows behind them, they entered a hermetically sealed bubble that the record company and management used to protect them from the demands of the outside world. Bon Jovi were now very big news and very big business and nothing could be allowed to get in the way of that. If they thought they'd been worked hard to get to this point, they hand't seen anything yet.

The *Slippery When Wet* tour eventually lasted a back-breaking sixteen months with over 200 shows in every part of the world. Jon was carried along on adrenalin, on the sheer excitement of finally having a hit record and the knowledge that he was now secure for life, able to continue a recording career for as he long as he should choose. He was never complacent, however, for he reminded himself that every night was special for the crowd, every night was the only night of the tour for each audience. His statements indicated his commitment to work and to himself:

I'm not satisfied, not at all. I would give anything, I would sell my soul ... like I'd give a day of my life for every day I can sing good – that's pretty sick but I've said that to myself. That's how much I dig it ... I dig it so much I'd give up everything and everyone I know. It is bad ... I'd kill my mother for rock'n'roll and that's sick. It's the weirdest sensation.

Not a statement to take at face value – though his mother might have decided to get some life assurance, or a bodyguard, after hearing it – it smacked a little of self-aggrandizement: Jon Bon Jovi the screwed up rock'n'roll casualty who lost his mind over the adulation. A little mythology and mystery goes a long way in the rock business, yet none could deny the almost evangelical zeal with which he approached the gigs. They were the central plank of his life, what he lived for; he was determined to make every show perfect, better than the last. His philosophy was simple, though worrying: 'I want to hurt myself, I want to break bones, I want to sweat and bleed. I want to make sure I'm the best I can possibly be. There've been nights which I've looked at Richie and he's thought I'm going to hit him. There's an intensity.'

As much as the crowd, Jon seemed addicted to that transcendent moment of which many performers speak and which is almost the equivalent of an out-of-body experience. Bono has talked about the difficulty in coming back down to earth after a concert tour, and Jon experiences much the same dilemma. Is it that these are people with enormous egos which require the constant boost of publicity or adoration? It seems unlikely in Jon's case, since away from the stage he doesn't court the press, tries to live a normal life and has none of the affectations of many 'stars'. What then is the attraction? Probably it's the affirmation that they are worthwhile as people, that their work is appreciated. His academic prowess being negligible, Jon must have been berated by teachers for not paying enough attention in school. Standing in front of 15,000 people all of whom hang on your every word is a powerful act of revenge against the system that sought to commodify you and turn you into a homogeneous unit.

He really does love the concert stage. On the *Slippery When Wet* tour he was in his element, but even he began to flag by the end of it all, his voice ripped to pieces: 'I'd hate to see what my throat looks like.' The show-must-go-on trooper in him kept pushing him on to the stage to give his all for the crowd: 'You just have to try and pick it up one more time. Whatever it takes.' In a perceptive article for *Sounds* in August 1987, Richard Cook noted, 'He is so tired but they can't let him stop yet. There may be another million records they could do. There must be more badges, more shirts, more trinkets to sell. It's a tour that could have stopped long ago, but it has to continue.'

Further fuel is given to that thesis by the statistics. A 130-date US tour in 1987 grossed $28,400,000. When that kind of money is rolling in, there's no time to stop and think. Advisers are pushing to play one more big show in a market that's just catching up; there's a festival here, a tour there. The man in the eye of the hurricane is so caught up in just keeping himself going that he doesn't have the time nor the energy to argue, but simply continues to drag himself through the stage door and on towards his public. The *Slippery When Wet* tour was a model of the financial exploitation of a hit record without a single thought for the consequences.

It is desperately difficult to keep your mind on all the peripheral tasks that have to be done to keep a band rolling when wrapped up in such an enormous project as Bon Jovi had become. Jon had given himself too much to do and in the end could do little more than say yes when Doc McGhee or a concert promoter asked a question. To add to his burden, there was now a huge organization all reliant on Bon Jovi for their income. Would they ever be as successful again? If not, surely now was the time to earn everyone a comfortable pension. Concerned with the financial welfare of the friends that were now employees, Jon could only resolve to work himself even harder, collapsing in an exhausted heap whenever he could find the time.

The demands of stardom also began to eat into him. He awoke to find people camping on his lawn on the few occasions he was at home, the tabloids became increasingly intrusive and their triumphal headlining return to the Monsters of Rock festival at Donington before 80,000 people was marred when a Brazilian fan collapsed and died. Further injuries were caused when tickets went on sale for a show in New York – seven people were trampled underfoot in the rush – while in San Antonio there were reports of fans being mugged for their tickets at gunpoint when even the touts had sold out. None of this was within Jon's control but it merely illustrated the crazy and chaotic times they were wrapped up in. More seriously, internal bickering intensified through sheer fatigue. The friendship remained intact but there was no denying that the five needed a break from one another. Reflecting later, all were agreed that they could barely remember any of the *Slippery* tour, the whole thing just one long blur.

With such vast sales behind them, you would be forgiven for thinking that all their troubles seemed so far away – but things are seldom that easy. A record that sold around 13 million copies within a year is cause for celebration, but there has to be a sense of proportion about the triumph. Once an album reaches that point, many many people are buying the record simply because it is popular, the success generating its own unstoppable momentum. To hit those statistics, you have to start selling albums at petrol stations and supermarkets to the casual buyers who get their music when they buy cornflakes. The core audience might be six or seven million – still pretty respectable – but the remaining millions cannot be considered loyal supporters. When you next have a record out they'll have moved on to that month's statistical freak. One nagging worry existed in Jon's mind: within the pages of the hard rock press there had been increasing disquiet, suggestions that Bon Jovi had betrayed their roots. Certainly the introduction of Desmond Child had firmly placed them in the AOR market alongside groups like Foreigner, Journey, Asia and GTR.

There is ample evidence of the loyalty of rock fans. But that loyalty is not elastic, and many wondered if Bon Jovi had sacrificed too much of their original sound in the pursuit of sales; certainly many of the rock fraternity felt that Richie had been sorely underemployed on *Slippery When Wet*. The scent of compromise was in the air and that is one thing that a rock fan does not care for. By the time Bon Jovi returned to Donington in August 1987, it was imperative that they re-established their rock credentials before their harshest critics, a feat they accomplished with aplomb. Dancing deftly from lite metal to hard rock, Jon recalled the great Phil Lynott in his performance, playing the 'rock star' to the hilt but always able to duck under the facade and let the crowd in on the joke. With Sambora given his head once again, Bon Jovi staunched the flow of criticism from the fans and rescued the core audience for the next offering. And yet ... '[that] was an example of the stupidity gamut,' Jon told:

> I was on steroids, I had grown a beard for two weeks, there were black circles under my eyes. We really shouldn't have done that. I was like 'Stop, please, I'm dying'. And they said 'we've still gotta go to Australia, to Europe again', and holy fuck I just wanted to crawl into bed and die'.

Something was rotten in the state of New Jersey.

A lesser concern came as the critical vultures began to circle. Pop had suddenly sprouted a moral and political conscience with the Amnesty International *Conspiracy of Hope* tour, artists playing benefits for ecological groups and so on. Jon was dismissed in some quarters as an airheaded throwback to the dinosaur days of heavy rock when the likes of Led Zeppelin pillaged their way across continents, singing about nothing more important than the size and potential uses to which they intended to put their genitalia. Having glorified rock's stupidity and its wild abandon early in 1986 as an antidote to Live Aid, this year's model was the sensible pop star. Jon was adjudged to be unsuited for the role, particularly in the light of 1987's other phenomenon, U2, who were touted as the rock group that wanted to save the world.

Understandably Jon let much of this criticism wash over him, pointing to the number of smiling faces at the concerts, but some of it stung. Unconvincingly, he posited that, 'We never set out to change the world – rock'n'roll to me was always entertainment. It wasn't a place to be talking about politics or nuclear holocausts. As much as I love U2 and Little Steven's my idol, it's like *you* write about that stuff, I ain't concerned.' This poor choice of words merely added fuel to the fire that Jon was an addle-brained hedonist who couldn't see further than the delights of a drink and a girl. Particularly in the post-AIDS climate and with the *Slippery* sleeve controversy still in people's minds, many felt Jon was behaving irresponsibly.

This opprobrium did little to alter his attitudes, though he later confessed that 'there are some pretty interesting diseases out there ... it's toned down quite a bit. Compared to what we used to do, man, it's like Sunday School now.' Politically there was evidence that Jon was taking a greater interest in the world around him; his reticence to speak out was as much a function of his unwillingness to be cast in the messianic role as his confusion as to what he could say. 'Livin' On A Prayer' was hardly a political manifesto but it did show that Jon was aware of the world beyond Bon Jovi – but as a novice, he was not prepared to make any outspoken statements that could be misconstrued. In all likelihood, with the emphasis on financial gain above any other considerations, he would have been counselled against saying anything that might be controversial and which could harm ticket sales.

Swamped by the success he now had, Jon became a prisoner of his own fame – not in the sense that he couldn't go out any longer, for his personality remained basically the same: unaffected, charming, pleasant. His cage was built by the money men who saw him as the golden goose. When *Slippery* eventually ran out of steam at the end of 1987, Bon Jovi looked forward to a long rest. They didn't get it.

7

THE JERSEY SYNDICATE

The days of being just a singer in a rock'n'roll band, packing up the station wagon and driving round the country, had long gone for Jon Bon Jovi. One of the pitfalls of success is that life has a habit of becoming increasingly complex in its wake; money brings more than its fair share of trouble. The obvious problems are how to save it, where to put it and how to ensure you pay your tax bills, but these are relatively simple little posers if you have a good, trustworthy accountant. The real predicament comes with the wealth itself – once you've got it, everybody else wants, and thinks they deserve, a piece of it. As with the lottery winner, as soon as Bon Jovi hit the jackpot the friends and relatives began to crawl out of the woodwork. Alec explained the trouble: 'you have all this "family" you never knew existed and surprise, surprise they're all down on their luck and need a few bucks.'

Rogue family members were one thing; the greater difficulty came with what might be termed Bon Jovi's extended family. No longer just another Polygram act, Bon Jovi had become a huge business in their own right with many jobs riding on their success. Jon had become the apex of an inverted pyramid, his voice, his songwriting, his personality and his performance holding everything else up. He needed some time to refresh himself after the *Slippery* tour, as did the rest of the band, but the financial demands just kept rolling in. They could quite easily have ignored them for they'd pulled in more money than they'd ever need, but both management and record company were afraid that a break now might undo all the hard work that had been done. To put it in perspective, on the *Slippery* tour, Bon Jovi played to four million people, each of whom spent more, on average, on merchandising than on their ticket. If Bon Jovi disappeared for a year the next album might only sell four or five million. Instead of nine or ten, they might only play to two million fans. Why not capitalize on a winning streak?

Jon managed to convince himself that it was a good idea to go back on the road, arguing that he needed the applause to keep him going: 'After a few days home you don't remember the tour, it's over, bang bang! You try and grasp some memories of it but you can't, they've gone too fast. So its like 'God, I need some more'. I become a junkie, I need another fucking fix.' Prior to another tour though they would have to write and record a new album, of which more in a moment.

There were very good financial reasons to justify the excessive demands placed on Jon and the band in 1988 and 1989, sadistic though they were. Jon, however, was not totally motivated by money. Certainly he enjoyed his wealth and he had begun to indulge the occasional rock star whim, buying Ferraris which sat unused and so on, but the money had only ever been a part of his motivation. Security assured, it was less and less important. The moral blackmail angle may have been tried by Polygram and McGhee, reminding Jon of his obligations to his staff and the need to make sure they all got a nice Christmas bonus in 1988. Many hard-nosed journalists have continued to testify to Jon's warm-hearted nature, so such pleas would have made a lasting impression, but that could only have been part of the story. There is one strain of opinion that suggests that external events were moving at too fast a pace to control and that other responsibilities were closing in on him. Just as in his youth, once the real world got to be too much for him, he escaped with a guitar in his hand.

Certainly 1988 had begun very badly indeed. In April, Doc McGhee was tried and convicted of marijuana smuggling, a case that went back to a 1982 seizure of nearly 40,000lbs smuggled into North Carolina from Colombia, prior to his association with Jon; given that that is the equivalent of 80,000 eight-ounce tins of hash, there was sufficient confiscated to keep a full Wembley Stadium in a very good mood for a very long time. As a result, he was fined $15,000, received a five-year suspended prison term and given extensive community service to perform. Continuing that great judicial tradition of moral bankruptcy in the face of rock's earning potential, McGhee bought off his community service by organising an anti-drug benefit album, the *Make A Difference Foundation*, something which he contrived to use to his own advantage as we shall see. This 'arrangement' was a feat of hypocrisy that equalled the Keith Richards fiasco in Toronto in 1978 when the human laboratory was found guilty of possessing heroin and escaped jail through the expeditious means of playing a benefit concert.

The ins and outs of the court case are beyond the province of this narrative. Certainly there is no suggestion that any member of Bon Jovi had any knowledge of Doc's dealings or benefited from them. However, McGhee had long had a slightly dubious reputation in rock circles and few were entirely surprised when the news broke; questions were asked as to whether other shady deals were being done behind Jon's back and whether this was the reason he was being worked so hard, keeping him out of Doc's way and keeping his books balanced. Certainly there has never been anything to lend weight to such allegations and any idle speculation on the matter would be malicious.

Jon's private reaction on hearing the news is anyone's guess – dismay and disgust are the most promising candidates – but in public he stood behind his manager. As one would expect from one who holds the family and the brotherhood ideal so dear, there was no way that Jon could or would take the soft option and dispense with Doc's services. He merely 'stood tall' as he put it and, just like in his favourite westerns, did what a man had to do, backing his friends to the hilt. Many big name managers made their overtures, trying to tempt him to transfer his allegiance, but he would have none of it. That is entirely in keeping with his credo, but it was a decision that was far from being in his best interests.

It can only ever be a matter of conjecture but in his conviction for a serious crime, Doc McGhee might ironically have extended his tenure with Bon Jovi by a couple of years. Although relations between manager and client seemed cordial enough, it was very definitely Doc who instigated the mammoth tours, it was he who kept Bon Jovi on the road in order to squeeze the last drop out of *Slippery When Wet* and he who demanded a rapid follow up. Constantly accelerating the speed at which the treadmill was turning, he never allowed Jon the time to stop and think about just what it was that he wanted to do with the next few months and years. Doc's principle seemed to be: keep the boy occupied and he won't ask any awkward questions. Did he really want to go through the same touring hell that he'd endured for the last 16 months? Did he want to go back into the studio again or did he instead fancy the idea of taking some time to relax, unwind and enjoy the wealth he had created? Richie admitted that he had missed the last half of the *Slippery* tour because he was in such a terrible physical and mental state. He was there onstage, but none of it sunk in; Jon must have felt the same way for he told '*Slippery* should have the best time of my life. But it wasn't. Things either happened too quickly or else I was physically exhausted trying to keep up with it all.' When in the course of a *Rolling Stone* interview Rob Tannenbaum jokingly suggested that after a trip to the virgin rock territory of Russia, they might look forward to their first jaunt to Mars, a visibly weary Jon replied, 'Don't say that in front of Doc. He'll have me up in the space shuttle.'

A musician takes on a manager for many reasons. It might be for his contacts in the music industry, it might be to arrange gigs or it might be to take charge of the administrative affairs; whatever the case, it is his prime function to keep the wheels of industry turning, to maintain the flow of money into the coffers for his charges and to keep them gainfully employed. By 1988 though, Doc McGhee seemed to have gone overboard on that last point. Whether Jon was beginning to have second thoughts about their relationship at this point is open to debate but his comments in Moscow as reported above suggest that cracks were beginning to appear. Things had moved at such a cracking pace that it might not have been feasible for Jon to change management or sack the Doc in the midst of this frenetic activity, though it's likely that there were times where the thought sprang to his mind. However, given Jon's very genuine belief in the 'brotherhood' which he now termed the 'Jersey Syndicate', once Doc fell into such deep trouble, he had to bale him out. There could be no question of severing the ties between the two; had the case not come to court, it is perfectly possible that Jon and Doc McGhee would have parted long before the 1991 split. By then, he had been able to pull McGhee out of the hole he'd dug for himself and then allowed sufficient time to pass to claim with justification that he was not dumping his manager because he'd become a liability. The two men had, by then, become further estranged, making Jon's decision very much simpler and more easily explained to the public.

The relationship between the two men was ludicrously simple – Doc was Jon's friend, so he would support him through thick and thin. On another level though, the association was complex. Each had a degree of obligation to the other; Jon was Doc's most successful client, the source of his income, so Doc had every reason to stay in his good books. At the same time, Jon recognized that, like Richie, Doc had proved to be a good partner, doing his job well and playing a full part in the Bon Jovi organization. The difficulty came once *Slippery When Wet* had been so successful, for their motives diverged. Jon no longer had to chase recording success for any financial reasons, he could choose to record or to take a long vacation safe in the knowledge that publishing and recording royalties would continue to flow into the bank account. For Doc, however, although still taking his percentage on such income, it was significantly lower than he might have liked. For him to earn substantial amounts of money, Jon had to keep working. In addition, while Bon Jovi were off the road, McGhee could not bask in the reflected glory, could not indulge his expansive personality in the full glare of the spotlight and could not maintain his high profile inside the music business. With Bon Jovi still a group of relatively young men enjoying their success, Doc's entreaties for the band to start work again as soon as possible were convincing. It also meant that Jon could escape the endless round of questions about his future with McGhee. He retreated into the studio and then escaped on to the road just as he had as a youngster.

In fairness to McGhee, Jon himself was something of a

workaholic; if we hark back to the principle of the American Dream that was covered earlier on, the chief characteristic of people pursuing that goal is their willingness to put the hours in. Coming to terms with just what he had done would have been difficult: from nobody to international superstar within six months. All those years trying to turn the dream into reality wouldn't have prepared him for the speed with which it arrived. There may have been some part of Jon that simply couldn't accept his good fortune. In consequence he would have continued to get up and go to work just in case the bubble burst; he was to complain that his parents wouldn't quit work once he'd become a multi-millionaire without any trace of irony. The work ethic was obviously passed down from one generation to the next.

He had always looked for some musical project to fill the time. He and Richie had already provided songs for Ted Nugent, Cher and Loverboy among others and Jon had also taken on the role of unpaid agent for glam-rockers Cinderella, helping them secure a contract and then taking them on the road. This was evidence that Jon had not forgotten his roots and the way in which he had been helped and inspired by other musicians back in New Jersey. These were little more than diversions though, for Jon's main preoccupation was still Bon Jovi.

Both he and Richie were in a particularly creative spell, as Jon noted. After the *Slippery* tour had finished, 'We really didn't do anything for 3 or 4 weeks, then the phone calls started to change from "whatcha doin' today?" to "I got this really neat hook!"' Having sold quite unbelievable quantities of records, they retained their ambition. With such success behind them, they were not content to rest on their laurels but instead were trying to build a platform for the future. While they were the proud owners of one of the most commercially successful records ever, they were a little upset by the reaction of critics. Many observers continued to dismiss them as pretty boy rockers writing simplistic, banal pop fluff, attributing their success to the advent of Desmond Child.

Those remarks rang in their ears, and they were desperate to prove that they were good songwriters, strong musicians who were responsible for their own accomplishments. The best way of doing just that was to come up with an even better record, though in the early stages this desire translated itself into an almost unbearable pressure:

> We demoed the first batch of songs, seventeen in all ... we really started to feel the pressure because we didn't have the *amazing* song. I panicked to be honest. I really wanted to do it again, not for the monetary reasons but it was such an amazing feeling to have done what we'd done ... and I'm walking round the house yelling 'I gotta pay for this place, we got write some fucking hot songs!'

A further charge that Jon wanted to answer was that made by certain hard rock fans that *Slippery When Wet* had been a pale shadow of their more robust early albums, a weak compromise in order to engineer some hit records. He wanted to show to the world that he had not gone soft but at the same time he was not prepared to pander to anyone else's agenda, nor their view of what Bon Jovi should be. So it was that just a few short months after completing touring duties in Hawaii, he was writing songs with Richie Sambora and looking to repeat the spectacular performance of the previous year and a half.

Yet he was a very different songwriter to the one he'd been in 1986. He and Richie were looking to work in a style similar to 'Wanted Dead Or Alive', a more articulate and mature piece compared with the rest of the material on *Slippery When Wet*. Richie was straining at the leash to play rather more guitar this time and Jon wanted to sharpen up his lyrics making them more personal and leaving behind the adolescent fantasies of the past. This change in style reflected Jon's own development as a man with wider interests than in days of yore. His reflections on the scouting trip they made to Moscow in early 1989 proved the point: 'We were only there for three days which isn't long enough to judge a country and its people. The strongest impression was what good people they were. They aren't the fucking baddies we were brought up to believe they were. That's all preconceived propaganda bullshit.' For a hard rock singer, this kind of statement was akin to political radicalism, though he went on to mar his new status by saying of George Bush, then American President, 'he's cool. I like George. I wanted to write him a letter after Russia to tell him what we'd done ... Mr Gorbachev and Mr Bush know it was an event and I headlined it.'

The obvious awe with which he spoke of being known to heads of State was, depending on your point of view, either touchingly or depressingly innocent, the sort of thing a child might have said. Among pop superstars who flaunted their narcissistic egos, carrying themselves as if they were the only thing that mattered in the world, his naivety and humble attitude were very appealing to a large section of the rock crowd who did not want to mix music and politics and who did want to believe in the intrinsic goodness of politicians; Bon Jovi too were able to cash in on a country that wanted proof of the virtues of the American Dream, the group supposedly embodying everything that was virile and vibrant about young America.

If anyone was in a position to be arrogant about his success it was Jon, but he refused to play that game, something which he put down to the influence of his parents. Dealing with money was a problem, but Jon knew where his responsibilities lay, as he told Q: 'to me it's as much [my parent's money] as mine. They're part of this ... they both work full-time still and they can't stop working. I told them 'I'll buy the god-damned business you work in if you'll just stop'. But they don't listen. They just tell me to shut up and remember where I come from.'

It was inevitable though that however hard Jon might try to stay in contact with friends and to retain the human touch, his new status had to carry him away from 'ordinary' life. The things that had happened to him on a business footing, allied to the experiences and people he had encountered on the road, meant that he had to lose that sense of wide-eyed innocence. As he became more and more concerned with the world beyond the confines of Bon Jovi, that loss of innocence turned to a dewy-eyed nostalgia for the simple life he had lived and the world he had known as a child. His buddies in school were a part of that world, but he could not always keep tabs on their movements. As anyone gets older, they slip apart from the people they grew up with as they each pursue their own lives. Jon had the added difficulty that old friends often found it hard to know how to deal with his success. These were the thoughts that were going through Jon's mind on returning home from the road a multi-millionaire and it was this that defined the direction which he wanted to pursue in his lyrics.

With Richie thinking along the same lines, the songs they began to write were tougher than on *Slippery* even if some had similarities. 'Wanted Dead Or Alive' was the launching pad for this new collection of songs, for it embodied a sense of Jon's kinetic lifestyle, his outlaw fixation and the emphasis which he placed on friendship, while musically there was an emotional charge to it that songs like 'Livin' On A Prayer' could not hope to approach for all their commercial attraction.

The more thought Jon gave to the things that meant the most to him, the more he came to realize that New Jersey was a vital part of him, the ingredient that made him the individual he was. It was with a rueful smile that he acknowledged the significance of the Garden State: 'When I was a kid all I wanted to do was get the fuck outta New Jersey! A one way ticket was all I could think about. It took me a coupla world tours to realise how much I longed to be with the people and places I know.' It was also the final admission that his flirtation with Hollywood and showbiz glamour was at an end. When on the road for the first time, he went off the rails, taken in by everything that fame had to offer. His salvation was to be found in his roots, a return to the values that his parents had passed on to him as a child. Dorothea was a part of that cycle too, their relationship split asunder by his fascination with the bright lights until he woke up and discovered that the important things in life were back home.

With this in mind, you might think that *New Jersey* was the only title under consideration for Bon Jovi's fourth album, but that was far from the case, as he admitted later:

The album was gonna be called *Sons of Beaches* and we had other titles like *Sixty Eight And I Owe You One* . . . all this nasty shit that was humorous in a way but it parodied *Slippery* and would have left us pigeonholed ... *Sons of Beaches* was great for the hands-up-in-the-air anthem stuff, but maybe it didn't say 'Christ these guys have got a helluva lot better at writing songs'. [*New Jersey*] is as close as we can get to saying 'make up your mind'.

It was a case of wiser counsel prevailing, for *New Jersey* was an infinitely better title than the lazy postcard humour of the other possibles. As a title it made a take-it-or-leave-it statement about the album; where *Slippery When Wet* was begging you to like it and take it home with you, *New Jersey* was indifferent. This was an album that the protagonists were entirely happy with and would not change in any way. They hoped you might like it and would do everything possible to sell you a copy but if at the end you weren't interested, they viewed it as your loss not theirs. After eighteen months of desperately trying to please all and sundry, such defiance was healthy and wholly justified, for *New Jersey* was a very good record indeed, infinitely superior to their previous albums. A mature body of work, it covered a breadth of emotional terrain, the playing was better than ever and Jon's voice was perfectly attuned to the material. As a potent illustration of the diverse music that he had enjoyed as a child and that he was still listening to – Jesus and Mary Chain for instance were an ostensibly incongruous fixture on the Bon Jovi stereo – *New Jersey* was first class. No longer forced into corners by marketing men with their explanations of demographics, market penetration and promotional campaigns, Bon Jovi were at a point where they could relax and enjoy themselves.

Musically freer than ever before, it was surprising to learn that Bon Jovi still had to conform to the wishes of the industry. When the songs did start to flow, Jon and Richie soon compiled around 30 from which to choose. Recording was set for May 1st to July 31st in Vancouver, with Bruce Fairbairn again at the helm, and things went so smoothly that Jon was keen to make it a double album, so strongly did he feel about the material in hand. However, 'Polygram wouldn't let us. They fought me tooth and nail from the minute I said it ... there wasn't much I could do about it.' When

Jon Bon Jovi, one of the most powerful artists in popular music, can't dictate terms, you begin to fear for the rest. Admittedly Polygram had reasons for their opposition; record stores don't like double albums, they are costly to produce, less profitable and with compact disc technology making its presence felt, the prospect of having to produce a double CD was daunting. In a more kindly moment, you might suggest that the company had Bon Jovi's best interests at heart – for how many really good double albums have there been? Very few, while most would have been improved by judicious pruning to normal length. Sadly, however, it's unlikely that the arguments were anything other than economic.

As it transpired, it was a good decision musically for it left the group with the space to use only the very best tracks and the record did benefit from that frugality, having few discernible weak links. Where it irrefutably scored over its predecessor was in the heartfelt honesty of its sentiments and the very personal lyrical stance that Jon took. Some choose to scoff at his old-fashioned belief in the bond between friends but it obviously meant the world to him, his Italian heritage still clearly an important motivating factor in his life.

Unfortunately, the 'brotherhood' could be taken a little too far, especially in the live show, and that did expose him to ridicule, as the *Guardian*'s Adam Sweeting was only too happy to point out: 'above all, he would have us know, the important things is the bond between people. And so it was that Jon and his band enacted a buddy ritual, gathering at the front of the stage to clasp hands and swear undying loyalty to each other. I was careful not to be sick over my shoes.' Sweeting then went on to dismiss the show as 'lots of hardware but not much heart', where if anything the fault lay in too obvious a display of heartfelt emotion.

All this talk of fidelity is sometimes hard to take at face value given Jon's behaviour elsewhere; by his own admission he was not faithful to Dorothea during the early days on the road. David 'The Snake' Sabo was unceremoniously ditched when Richie Sambora, admittedly a more compatible songwriter and guitarist, came on the scene. As we will see later, Jon split with Doc McGhee and there were reports of acrimonious group meetings when he threatened to end the band; there were serious accusations of contractual impropriety after he helped launch Skid Row's career and, finally, Alec Such went on the record with some very harsh comments about the way Jon had treated him. There is good reason then to doubt just how loyal Jon is to others when it conflicts with his own interest, so the 'Jersey Syndicate' ideal has to be regarded somewhat sceptically.

One bond that does appear to be unbreakable, however, is that between him and his audience. There really doesn't seem to be anything he wouldn't do to ensure his crowd has a great night out, as this story shows: 'I played with a fractured leg for about six weeks of [the *New Jersey*] tour but it was just from over-use I guess. I broke it onstage, I cracked the tibia and I got it taped up so I could still bounce around on it.' Springsteen (him again) once commented, 'going to where the people are, going to their towns, that's always been the thing with me. You want to cut down on that distance between the audience and the guy makin' the record . . . it's its own reward.' The Boss can get away with that kind of statement for people generally and genuinely believe that he is being honest; a man who started out as a singer in a hard rock band is rarely given that benefit of the doubt, a point forcibly made by Steve Turner in a review of the 1989 Wembley Arena shows in *The Times*: 'Bon Jovi music can only really work for you if you believe in the Bon Jovi myth. If you don't believe you are left with the sound of one man worshipping himself in the mirror of an audience and an audience worshipping itself in the mirror of a man.'

Turner's point holds water – if you don't believe in the veracity of the escapist, optimistic world that Jon Bon Jovi seeks to create, the band's music will appear hollow and calculated. Yet apply Turner's point to the world's more credible acts and the same is true; if you don't believe in U2's vision of social and political compassion, if you don't believe in Springsteen as everyman, if you don't believe in Michael Stipe's engagingly eccentric persona, then they too could be dismissed as glory hunters. But Bon Jovi were an out-and-out heavy rock group at the outset and few critics were subsequently willing to listen to them with an unprejudiced ear.

Had they done so, *New Jersey* might have been a pleasant

surprise for it was the culmination of the artistic growth that had begun in earnest on *Slippery When Wet*. One grave criticism that could be levelled at it, however, was that in sequencing it suggested a formulaic desire to follow on from *Slippery When Wet* and that success. *New Jersey* opened with 'Lay Your Hands On Me' a song that shared many stylistic similarities with 'Let It Rock' which had ushered *Slippery* in. That had been followed by 'You Give Love A Bad Name', the huge hit; for *New Jersey* track two was 'Bad Medicine', the huge hit. Little wonder that those who lacked faith in Bon Jovi's ability to surprise gave up at that point, for though these were superior rewrites, they were rewrites none the less.

The album continued to mirror this mood that saw them caught between two stools – following the advice of industry moguls to capitalize on their reputation with a record in the same vein as *Slippery* on one hand, while on the other attempting to maintain their own interest in the record by stretching the sound in new directions and applying new visions. It could have led to an unholy mess, but to their credit Jon and Richie managed to hold it all together for most of the time.

'Lay Your Hands On Me' was a reflection on the way their world had changed in the wake of multi-platinum success, Jon telling *Sounds* that 'people perceive us as this band that's bigger than life and we wanted to say, "hey, things are going well but you can still touch us!"' Designed for the concert arena pure and simple, its raucous drum intro made for an obvious set opener and made it plain that Bon Jovi weren't going to become a synthesizer group or an acoustic band overnight; changes were planned, radical ones compared with hard rock norms, but the fans could still rely on them to deliver a good time. Was this playing it safe, should they be pandering to the fans or should they not use their position to expose the crowd to wider influences? These were questions asked with monotonous regularity but that is to misunderstand the reasons for Bon Jovi's existence. They operate in a genre that for 'serious' critics is beyond the pale. To them, hard rock is a style that is cliché stacked upon cliché, but to its adherents it's just a component part of a good night out, entertainment pure and simple with no other agenda attached. The fanbase knows what it likes and likes what it knows and is adamant that that's what it wants. To stray too far from the path would have meant the decimation of their audience, too high a price for a band that had only just found its crowd.

Jon had artistic ambitions but above all, as an ebullient, virile young man, success had become addictive; it was his biggest goal and he was not going to jeopardize the chance of another hit from that heady drug. He confessed that 'There's no high like knowing you can do Madison Square Gardens just in a fucking phone call. It's ludicrous. A dream.' Reflecting on a show at the Budokan in Japan that hadn't sold out, he asserted 'You'd give all that money back to fill a hall, money don't mean shit!' Such vociferous claims can usually be put down to a star with an eye on some good press coverage of his lack of materialism, but with Jon they sounded surprisingly honest, as he continued by saying, 'We've made a lot of money and I don't have to work any more but if you offered me $100 million to stop doing this I'd tell you to keep the money. This is such a fucking high it's an addiction.' In making such a proclamation, he was revealed as either a very practised liar or a sick man, needing the love of the crowd more than the financial backing to make him and his family secure forever. None of the pat cod-psychological theories fit – he had a very warm family background and so wasn't looking for the love he didn't get at home, and he rejected school before it rejected him so his career could only ever be a limited act of revenge. Why did he need success so badly?

'I am competitive, everybody is' he explained, yet that hardly does justice to his determination to fill stadiums everywhere. At the age of 26, Jon Bon Jovi was not an old man even in rock'n'roll terms so he would have had few worries that time was running short. Sufficiently intelligent to understand that *New Jersey* would be unlikely to match the sales figures of *Slippery When Wet*, he knew that he would be in for a bruising time on its release – not quite the reassurance he would appear to have been seeking. Why put himself through the performing hoop once again?

The most logical answer appears to lie in his outlaw obsession; its basic premise of riding into town, stealing the girls and the money and riding out again was its main attraction for him – the perpetuation of a childhood dream. But what did it represent to him? Its allure was in its escapist connotations: a lifestyle that enabled him to remain frozen in permanent adolescence, a second childhood that kept him and the band immune to all the bad news that bombarded the rest of the world. By denying that he was part of the 'normal' world, he could deny that anything had changed since the blood brother rituals he had gone through as a youngster. He could deny the responsibility that he had to his many employees as the head of the Bon Jovi empire, he could refuse, quite legitimately, to take any interest in the world beyond rock'n'roll and he could refuse to grow up. Bon Jovi Land was essentially Never Land where Jon could be feted as the irresponsible yet charming Peter Pan. In his denials of the existence of the adult world, he could climb back under the secure and protective blanket of an idyllic, idealized childhood, a childhood this time without school but with money and with the admiration of his peers, approval that was renewed on a nightly basis.

The simplistic, generous view of life was reaffirmed in 'Blood on Blood', a song wrapped in the cloak of brotherhood, the characters real friends from his childhood. Understandably nostalgic for a particularly enjoyable time of his life, Jon was keen to stress its importance to him:

> I think me and Richie both want people to remember us for this song, for 'Wanted', for that kinda tune . . . it's just things that I'll never forget, about those few years in my life from 12 or 13 until I was like 17. [Me and my friends] were inseparable and we really experienced all the things of growing up together.

The narrative rings true yet it simultaneously exposes the myth of loyalty, something which he seemed unwilling to accept. Without any sense of the irony of the situation, while explaining the song to reviewers he admitted that he'd lost contact with Bobby and Danny. The more he argued in favour of lifelong friendship, the more it sounded like a man trying to convince himself rather than anyone else.

Along with 'Born To Be My Baby' and the vocal performance on 'Living In Sin', 'Blood on Blood' carried an obvious debt of gratitude to Springsteen and the E Street Band. But again the criticism raised its head – Jon's songs spoke of the world as he'd like it to be, maybe as it should be, while Springsteen generally concluded his songs with a grain of gritty, unpalatable realism. Superficially, 'Blood on Blood' covers similar ground to 'No Surrender' from *Born In The U.S.A.* but where Bon Jovi are all defiance, Springsteen ends on a wistful note that accepts changing times and the fact that life can get in the way of ideals. It's a subject that colours much of Springsteen's work and makes a useful contrast to Jon's almost obsessively upbeat philosophy.

'Born To Be My Baby' was a central song on *New Jersey* according to a *Sounds* interview: 'I guess that's a lot of what the album is to do with – friendship. Okay, 'Born To Be My Baby' may be boy and girl but it's not sexual, it's more about friends.' Despite the smoke-screen, this was a personal song that had much to do with his relationship with Dorothea and the advanced stage that was reaching. In itself, this was a further indication of his maturity; he was beginning to discover that trust and friendship were far more important ingredients than the physical aspect, yet there was rarely any hint that such relationships can and do break down. As with the determined histrionics of the obligatory ballad, the Beatles-influenced 'I'll Be There For You', there was no admission of vulnerability – and yet Jon had had failed liaisons with both Dorothea and Diane Lane and so had plenty of source material on which to draw. Though the Springsteen comparisons may wear thin, if you stand these two songs against 'Downbound Train' from *Born In The U.S.A.* or 'Stolen Car' from *The River* you are left in no doubt as to who was the more formidable artist, who has the emotional depth to capture a snapshot of the real world. Jon's love songs were shamelessly romantic and, consequently, hugely popular yet the other side of the coin was not often explored. His explanation for these songs was trite yet sincere: 'the lyrics are about loyalty, that kinda bond. It's pretty hip, loyalty's sorta like a tattoo; it's forever.'

To underline his new-found loyalty towards Dorothea, he got a tattoo and got married on the same day on 28 April 1989. Talking to *Smash Hits*, he illustrated just how important romance was to him, his proposal coming in the wake of a successful show at the Los Angeles Forum: 'we went out and got very drunk in Las Vegas, went to a tattoo parlour and got myself a new tattoo, went gambling in a casino and won lots and lots of money and I said 'hey! Let's get married!' So we went and we did that and then got back to the hotel before the bar closed.' Such a grasp of priorities. The service took place at the Graceland Chapel at 11.45pm with no friends or family in attendance. The bizarre circumstances notwithstanding, that Jon should have finally tied the knot was very significant on a number of fronts.

It gave the signal that, having had to take on economic responsibility for his employees, he was now willing to take on a similar emotional obligation. He had lived an adult life that was devoid of any commitment other than to his audience, but now he gave notice that there were other, even more important matters to be dealt with. The timing did not go unnoticed either, midway through the *New Jersey* tour. If it wasn't going to turn the tour into a swan-song – for it was obvious that Jon would have to come back for a fix of applause sooner or later – it did intimate that he was tiring of the intense schedules and was looking to take more care of himself, mentally and physically. His marriage gave the clearest indication yet that Jon Bon Jovi was ready to grow up.

In the light of another song on the new album, these nuptials were all the more surprising. 'Living In Sin' was a track that Jon described as being 'a real personal, heartfelt song. It's as close as this white boy's ever come to soul!' Going on to say that it reflected where he stood at that point in his life, it was the most revealing track, effectively an anti-Catholic tirade. His confusion over his Roman Catholic background has already been touched upon – his antipathy for the way in which it is indoctrinated in children as the only faith and so on. Here though it was a mixture of revulsion and complete incomprehension at the petty nature of the church's rules that got under his skin. The lyric suggested that he had been taking some flak for not making an 'honest woman' of Dorothea; the archaic phrase 'living in sin' is a narrow-minded condemnation of people who live together but are not married by those who are hidebound by shallow convention. In his most substantial lyric, Jon attacked the moral bankruptcy of such arguments: how could anyone accuse a couple who loved each other and who lived happily together as 'sinful' simply because they had refused to take vows in front of a church full of hypocrites?

On reviewing *New Jersey* in *Q*, Marc Cooper noted that 'ballads like 'Born To Be My Baby' and 'I'll Be There For You' are positively Italian in their unblushing commitment and extreme promises.' It may have been this Italian heritage that pushed him down the aisle – if they are a warm and generous people, their arguments can be every bit as passionate; in addition it is expected that children will honour their parents and do the right thing by them. Constant pressure might well have eventually eroded Jon's resolution to remain a bachelor to the point where all he could do in protest was take the plunge in his own fashion.

Analysing *New Jersey* is a contradictory task; at once Bon Jovi have to be congratulated for expanding their repertoire, taking more risks than was probably wise and producing such a good record in such a short space of time, yet it is also an infuriating record in many respects. It promises more than it achieves, they don't stretch themselves as far as they could, should and, perhaps, would like to have done, and almost all the songs return to this theme of blind optimism or at best a refusal to accept a dark truth, shrouding it with wistful nostalgia for a better time. Jon continually backtracked to his own past to find an excuse for donning the rose-tinted specs: 'what I always got from rock'n'roll as a kid was the dream of something bigger and better ... I wanna bring people a little smile ... if you're not optimistic, you're dyin'.'

Such generous-spirited music was indeed rare and all the more welcome because of that, but as he began to show an aptitude for articulate, intelligent lyrics, it was disappointing that he did not choose to address the other aspects of the world around him. A case in point was '99 In The Shade'. Reflecting on the New Jersey coastline and days spent on the beach as a child, it was written as a reaction to news stories that hypodermic needles were being washed up on to the shore and, because of fears over the AIDS virus, the beach was closed down. That didn't necessarily require a political manifesto in song, yet '99 In The Shade' might at least have contained some reference to this ecological disaster so that the audience would have had an idea what had triggered this piece of reflection, and might be stirred to some kind of environmentally friendly action themselves. It may be asking too much that a song should help clear up the world's problems but it could be a link in a chain reaction that can improve general awareness of global issues.

Jon would have none of this, citing a conversation with Steven Van Zandt as confirmation that he was doing the right thing: 'Little Steven once said to me, "I'll save the world you save the kids" ... personally I don't want to sing about those things. I hope our contribution is to make people happy so that they take that attitude into tomorrow and don't go and shoot someone in a traffic-jam.' Perhaps he's right, but it seems more likely that by writing a 'green' song you might just motivate the concerned people in the Bon Jovi crowd to find out a little more about the world around them, whereas simply playing a good-natured song, however entertaining, however enjoyable, seems a pretty unlikely method of disarming a gun-toting maniac.

Writing '99 In The Shade' was a kind of therapy for Jon and Richie, as they recalled the balmy days of their youth and commented on

the end of an era, the end of the romanticism of the beach, of being able to go there in the summer with your kids or your girlfriend. It seems that the world's becoming a shitty place these days and that romanticism and loyalty are real important to me ... if I don't ever have a chance to go to the Jersey shore again I wanna remember it the way I did as a kid ... cotton candy and sausage sandwiches and bikinis and winning a record on the board-walk ... I'd be the first guy to donate money to a cause to help fix it up but I'm not gonna reflect that in my songwriting right now. I don't want to think about the bad shit that's happening to it now.

For a professional musician, Jon had a healthy disregard for his own importance. Recognizing that however hard he tried everything he did ended up as radio fodder, he accepted that 'my whole life is in those songs and yet when people are driving in the car they just flick through the channels. You turn us on and you turn us off . . . ultimately rock'n'roll is just entertainment . . . Joe Public just turns on the radio to get from Point A to Point B in the car.' Beliefs such as these have helped Jon Bon Jovi maintain a pretty level head through all the madness that he has been exposed to since becoming a household name and famous face. Although they ensure that he remains a genuinely decent man – stories that seek to assassinate his character are very scarce – they might be his Achilles heel too.

Inside the Bon Jovi camp, it's plain that Jon calls the shots and insists that those around him meet his exacting requirements, but even then he's careful not to trample on too many toes and tries very hard to run a happy ship. It's not always possible of course, for disputes and arguments always occur when people are working in a concentrated environment for long hours, but there does appear to be plenty of give and take. Allied to his addiction to success, this down-to-earth nature may have held him back from fully realizing his considerable musical potential. Studying a record like *New Jersey* at close quarters, it soon becomes clear that only a songwriter of uncommon gifts could have produced it; this is not to ignore the contribution of Richie and the rest of the group, but simply an observation that Jon is responsible for the genesis of most of the material and it is his stamp that is most clearly left on it. Each song is impressive in its own way, each could go in a variety of directions, each could stand alone from the parent album and have something to offer and yet each is restrained in some way.

Historically, most great, mould-breaking rock'n'roll music has been made at the extremes of the contemporary style – Elvis Presley was initially an extremist, The Beatles came to be extremists, Hendrix was born, lived and died an extremist, the rapid rise and untimely demise of Jane's Addiction was a consequence of their extremes of character and musical inspiration. Trent Reznor of Nine Inch Nails is another extremist currently producing some of the most innovative and influential music around. Very recently, Jon has gone on record to commend his work and suggest that they get together in the studio, while at the same time saying that he could never make records like Reznor's that and wouldn't have Nine Inch Nails as support, even if they were to accept such an offer. Although he has an affinity for other kinds of music and though he has a far greater breadth of vision than he ever chooses to display, the only conclusion is that Jon Bon Jovi has sacrificed possible greatness for comfort, mainstream success and an enjoyable lifestyle.

Many fans of the band will argue that Bon Jovi are the greatest. It is the audience's prerogative, but it cuts no ice. To enter the pantheon, an artist has to rank with those listed above – with Dylan, Springsteen or Costello. Yet while the fans clamour for Jon to be allowed into the Hall of Fame, the wider public, certainly the critics, will refute such claims with something approaching utter disbelief. Jon Bon Jovi, the pretty boy singer with a hard rock group, a great songwriter? Surely some mistake. The critics would be right, for he does not deserve that kind of respect as yet, but they would be wrong in not allowing for the depth of his songwriting skill, which he has left sadly neglected, untapped perhaps for fear of failing, of over-reaching himself and losing what he already holds.

No less a connoisseur than Elvis Costello called 'Bad Medicine' the 'best song on the radio' in 1988. Understandably thrilled, and with some justification, Jon called that the 'biggest compliment I ever received' for Costello knows a thing or two about great songwriting. On the surface, because of its enormous commercial value, 'Bad Medicine' is the kind of song that it's very easy to dismiss as pop fluff, but there is more substance to it than just that. Again written with the assistance of Desmond Child as well as Sambora – 'Born To Be My Baby', 'Wild Is The Wind' and 'Blood on Blood' were the other collaborations – it was as good an example of catchy late-eighties rock as you could hope to find. The lyric was sharp and witty, 'real tongue-in-cheek like the way we wrote "Social Disease"', an updating of the Bobbie Gentry hit 'I'll Never Fall In Love Again'. The real triumph came in the structure of the chorus. Whatever your opinion of Bon Jovi it was so cunningly crafted that even the most fervent opponents of the band found themselves singing along with it, a feeling akin to being mugged by a smiling thug. Infernally memorable, 'Bad Medicine' carried all the hallmarks of truly effective pop music at its best and it was no surprise when it became another American number one.

Such an obvious hit must have instilled confidence in the band, for the rest of the songs were a little more expansive and not so determinedly aimed at chart activity when compared with those on *Slippery When Wet*. Two tracks almost didn't make it on to the record until Jon went through the pizza parlour jury once more. 'This time,' Jon remarked, 'the kids picked a coupla songs, 'Stick To Your Guns' and 'Wild Is The Wind' that wouldn't have been on the record otherwise. I was gonna hold those songs off for the next record.' The reasons for holding 'Stick To Your Guns' back were not readily apparent, for thematically it dovetailed neatly with the rest of the material and it certainly didn't appear to be a new direction. It was another western epic of defiance mixed with the 'New Jersey' attitude; as Jon conceded 'we're cowboys at heart! It's probably not even the way real cowboys lived but it's our picture of it, more like a Clint Eastwood movie . . . when you do something you fucking better mean it!' To that extent, the song had a thread of autobiography in it inasmuch as Jon and the band always gave 100% of their energy to whatever project they had in hand – their defining characteristic. The cowboy analogies were becoming a little threadbare by this stage, however, so it's inclusion on the next Bon Jovi record would have been needlessly repetitive.

'Wild Is The Wind' was rather more of a pointer towards the future, as Jon freely admitted: '[it was] written when we were writing 'Blood on Blood'. We wanted to write a couple of long form songs . . . something more structured and with more of a lyrical content.' Opening with a burst of acoustic guitar that was reminiscent of Yes's Steve Howe, thereby exposing Richie's interest in progressive rock, it was an innovative take on the Bon Jovi format. The aura of disenchantment and defeat that pervaded the lyric struck exactly the right note of realism that the overly sentimental cuts such as 'I'll Be There For You' lacked; it repeated the first adult attempt at tackling loss, and was played and sung with total conviction. It stood out from the remainder of the album in the same way that 'Wanted Dead Or Alive' had on *Slippery When Wet*, boding well for future work.

The other two 'proper' songs on the album – 'Ride Cowboy Ride' was little more than an introductory doodle – gave the band a chance to have a little fun with their positon. 'Homebound Train' made it abundantly clear that Richie remained a Jimmy Page aficionado, the Zeppelinesque introduction and locomotive riff demanding accompanying vocal histrionics from Jon, who rose to the challenge and produced a nice approximation of Robert Plant.

The last song, 'Love For Sale' ended the record on an amiable note, creating the sought-after 'feel good' factor. Little more than a polished demo recording, it provided a nice example of the group at work and the interaction that took place between them during a session. Jon explained that 'we decided to put an eleventh song on the album, one because we wanted to add a little humour but besides that we wanted to let people get inside the band a little . . . it's supposed to be fun but it's also supposed to let you know what we do when we're not working.' The on-going dialogue at the end of the take was good humoured and designed to prick any incipient pomposity that surrounded their image as ultra-cool rock stars. Ironically, it highlighted all the difficulties that faced Bon Jovi; it was at once one of the choicest cuts on the record because of its unaffected warmth, yet it provided a glaring example of their refusal to reach out towards greatness. 'Love For Sale' was pleasant enough for fans yet history would judge it as just another good time tune from just another good time band, causing Mark Cooper to note that '*New Jersey* is so cheerfully romantic that it's as likeable as *Raiders of the Lost Ark* and almost as funny.'

Jon's reluctance to push himself as hard artistically as he did physically to fulfil his schedule remains a puzzle. Ambition was never in short supply, for he viewed each commercial milestone as something to be improved upon next time around, so why was he so musically conservative? Perhaps the first part of the sentence answers the question: despite his protests to the contrary, despite his constant demands to be regarded with respect as a songwriter, maybe the only reward that really meant anything came with the sound of chiming cash registers. You can make an argument that says 17 million Bon Jovi fans can't be wrong but sales do not tell the whole story – if they did then Barry Manilow would be a greater artist than John Lennon. It's as if Jon was frightened to take a leap into the unknown, scared of upsetting his loyal following with some radical shake-up of his musical principles. What does a man profit if he should make a truly great record that only sells 350,000 copies? Self-respect and artistic credibility might be enhanced but the fans would feel betrayed. Eight million fans constitute a substantial security blanket; he seems loath to risk the loss of that in the hunt for artistic satisfaction. The paradox can be summed up in the respective sales of *Slippery When Wet* – enjoyable but hardly a work of genius – and Costello's *Blood and Chocolate*, an astounding album released at the same time and peaking at 84 in the US album chart. For all the bold sentiments, Jon seemed happy to plough a furrow for substantial financial reward.

The pizza parlour jury only served to underline that message. Find out what the kids want and then give it to them is hardly the best way of ensuring ground-breaking creativity. On first exposure to a piece of music, we all like something with which we feel comfortable; the very best artists provide material with which we are unfamiliar yet which intrigue us sufficiently so that we go on to acquire the taste and discover something truly original, maybe learning something about ourselves on the way. Bon Jovi remained an enjoyable rock'n'roll band. There's nothing wrong with that unless you aspire – or pretend to aspire – to wider horizons.

According to their statements in the press, there were greater glories for Bon Jovi to reach, though when suggesting that 'Stick To Your Guns' was a song that pointed the way ahead, the story seemed less inspiring. Nevertheless Jon summed up the present and the future thus:

Our next album will be very experimental, it will be our *Sergeant Pepper*. We're gonna build it around two songs from the *New Jersey* sessions that were just so left-field for us ['Stick To Your Guns' and 'Wild Is The Wind'] . . . there may be more reflection on the next album, it'll go deeper in thought and feeling. But what matters to me now are the lyrics on these new songs. That's about as personal as I can get, I can't tell you any more about myself and still rhyme it! I'm not gonna tell you about pollution and the ozone layer and the President. It's not what I think about every day. We're television man! There's more substance in the Cosby Show.

Scarcely an admission designed to win new credibility for the band, yet in the face of 'Wild Is The Wind' it seemed reasonable to extend the benefit of the doubt for the moment at least.

Before there was to be any new *Sergeant Pepper* though, the *New Jersey* tour stretched seventeen months into the future. The opening night came in Dublin at the end of October 1988. Things were fraught enough already but the world's press descended on Dublin to hail the return of last year's conquering heroes and to see if they could still cut the mustard. Various reports reflected on Jon's manic behaviour prior to the gig; while support act Lita Ford was still onstage, Jon reputedly threw open the door of his dressing room to scream 'Get the bitch off! I'm on fire!' There was equal concern about the state of his trousers, which were appallingly sexist even by the towering standards of tawdriness that rock has set itself – they featured a naked woman painted on one leg, her hand reaching inside the fly, possibly accounting for his new falsetto.

Later he admitted,

> I dreaded this moment up until about two months ago. I hated it towards the end of the last tour. I was tired and I love going out there but I hated it. It almost killed me and I didn't realise because you just run on adrenalin ... I look at the pictures that were taken then and realise how sick I was. But I've really gotten in shape for this physically and mentally ... I was thinking 'you do this for a living, you can't get sloppy about it'.

Pausing only to question why, if he hated the previous tour, did he willingly embark on a similar trek within less than a year, the show itself is worthy of consideration.

This time around, the emphasis was placed on the songs rather than any instrumental virtuosity or flashy special effects. Certainly there were dramatically staged set pieces, Jon flying above the heads of the crowd to sing 'I'll Be There For You', giving a brief visual representation of his Peter Pan persona, but things were toned down from the over-the-top extravaganza that had accompanied the *Slippery* tour. Its effectiveness *was* determined by how far each individual bought into the Bon Jovi dream but generally there were 10,000 or more punters who went home happy each night.

'World Tours' generally refer to the USA and Europe, perhaps Japan and Australia too if they're lucky, but Jon and, more especially, Doc McGhee were looking to cover the whole world this time. Moscow was high on the agenda, ostensibly because of Doc's obligation to fund the anti-drugs foundation as part of his prison sentence. Jon and Richie already had some contact with the Soviet Union, having helped native metal band Gorky Park write some English lyrics, so they were only too happy to play a festival over there to raise money for the cause. They were one component of a bill that included Mötley Crüe, The Scorpions, Ozzy Osbourne, Skid Row and Gorky Park; to fit the supposedly selfless nature of the event, there were no plans to have a headline band as such, but Bon Jovi were to go on last as the best known band.

Inevitably this caused some ill feeling, especially since McGhee managed some of the other outfits. Mötley Crüe were especially enraged, bass player Nikki Sixx going on to complain that 'Bon Jovi tried to undermine things with pyrotechnics and lasers. We were very disheartened that there wasn't like this 'brotherly' thing. We felt we were getting second rate treatment from our manager so we sacked him.' The stories mushroomed into salacious tales of fisticuffs breaking out between Jon and Mötley Crüe drummer Tommy Lee, but Jon quickly tried to calm the atmosphere. In public he stood up for his manager once again, commenting that Mötley Crüe were complaining purely because they needed free publicity to help promote their new album and that he and Doc were sitting targets. Certainly he was willing to put his traditionally optimistic spin on the festival itself, telling *Sounds* 'I thought it was a great idea. It was a Godsend because it turned around something that was bad and hit millions of people with a message.'

Privately, however, this fiasco marked another staging post on the road to the final disintegration of his relationship with Doc McGhee. Rumours circulated as to how much money had been raised and where it went to, but from Jon's point of view the most serious issue was that Doc had hijacked the cause and the band for his own ends. *New Jersey* was the first album by a western band to gain a release in the Soviet Union on the state-run Melodiya label. A nice piece of history in itself, but financially useless since they received the maximum royalty of $9,600. However, as a businessman with an eye on the main chance, McGhee was working on the premise that if the political reforms were seen through to a conclusion, the Soviet Union would suddenly become an enormous rock'n'roll market-place. The first band to make an impact there would win the gratitude and the money of a nation. He manipulated the Make A Difference festival so that it became effectively a Bon Jovi show, to ensure that the Soviets would remember Bon Jovi above all else. McGhee was smart enough to realize that Bon Jovi were the band most likely to continue successfully into the next decade, so he promoted them for his own self-interest – or so the story goes. Certainly he was not too upset when Mötley Crüe severed their ties with his organization, for he still had Jon's business on his books.

It's a recurring theme throughout this tale, but in 1989 Jon was so busy he scarcely had time to take in the implications of Doc's dealings and the way in which the Moscow show had been rigged. Further problems were lying in wait too. At Jon's suggestion, Doc had signed up another New Jersey band, Skid Row, who featured David Sabo as guitarist, the man who had preceded Richie Sambora in Bon Jovi. A harder sounding band than Bon Jovi, Jon naturally took an interest in the work that his old friend was doing and, wary of all the pitfalls that could open up before a young and naive band on the way up, offered to help out. The arguments that eventually arose between the two bands came about because of the business footing that the arrangement was placed on.

Helping out in the studio, touting their name around record companies and so on, Jon was doing a great deal of work for Skid Row in his unofficial capacity. Having Jon Bon Jovi as guardian angel was an advantage that many a young band would have given anything to have, for it was tantamount to a guarantee of success, at least in the short term. Considering the work he was putting in on their behalf, Jon felt that he and Richie, who was equally involved, were entitled to financial reward. No-one is suggesting that there's anything wrong in this in itself, though one might argue that the main songwriters from a band who by the end of 1989 had sold almost 30 million albums were hardly short of a bus fare home; on the other hand it's fair to say that they were entitled to recompense for their labours. The bone of contention arose over how they were to be paid.

Doc McGhee was manager of both groups and apparently it was left to him to sort out the financial and contractual niceties. This alone smacks of extreme stupidity on the part of Jon and Richie and of Skid Row, for there was clearly a severe conflict of interests; obliged to get the best deal for all parties, how could McGhee drive a hard bargain with himself? Once the dust had settled, the facts became clear: Skid Row had signed away their music publishing rights on their first album to Jon and Richie. Since their eponymous debut album achieved sales in excess of three million copies, this was a tidy sum. Embarrassed by the revelations, Richie handed back his share to Skid Row, but Jon held on to his money.

The entire situation is thoroughly bizarre. Did Doc McGhee deliberately sell out one of his clients to the benefit of another? If so, he was guilty of professional misconduct and could have been dragged through the courts. Since this did not happen and since Skid Row are still managed by McGhee, one can only assume that this was not the case and that all parties were fully aware of the deal they were entering into. The idea that someone as obsessive about his own career as Jon would have simply got into the habit of signing contracts without scrutinizing them is rather far-fetched, so one has to assume that he knew what he was doing too. Perhaps he couldn't believe his luck that Skid Row were dumb enough to sign their rights away and that he naively felt this would be a good way of teaching them the same harsh lesson that he'd been taught by Tony Bongiovi back at the Power Station. Perhaps he felt that they didn't have real potential as a band and that the money involved was going to be negligible and so not worth worrying about. Or possibly he believed that by not taking any money up front but agreeing only to share in any success that they might have, he was helping out by not putting a strain on their initial resources; as the album sold, they would have earned substantial performing royalties as well as revenue from concerts, merchandising and so on and so could afford to reward him for the effrot he'd put in on their behalf. Put simply, if Skid Row had flopped, Jon wouldn't have made anything either, so, as far as he was concerned he was simply taking a commission earned by his successful promotion of the band. Certainly, without his patronage it's unlikely they would have become so big so quickly and Jon might have legitimately felt entitled to the reward.

If so, he was badly advised, for it made him seem like a ruthless businessman who had lost sight of reality, a surrogate company executive with no credibility. A figure of $2 million was bandied about as being his cut from the *Skid Row* record. As one of America's most successful rock stars ever – but a man who often said he didn't do things for monetary reasons – the Skid Row affair tarnished his reputation for it simply didn't fit in with his projected image. Jon Bon Jovi was instantly reported as a money-grabber who put the future of another band in jeopardy, while the oath of loyalty was further exposed as a myth.

This whole business was a sad end to the *New Jersey* experience which had been another high in the Bon Jovi story. As well as playing in the Soviet Union, they had headlined their own festival at the Milton Keynes Bowl in England, going on to play 237 shows in total in front of awestruck crowds. Far from losing popularity as a reaction to the global domination of *Slippery When Wet*, Bon Jovi had maintained their commercial pre-eminence in the rock world. Such was their fame that Jon was finally able to persuade his parents to give up work and move to a new home. Never one to miss a business opportunity though, he sold his childhood home to MTV who gave it away as a competition prize in March 1989, the same month in which the band were given the keys to the city at a homecoming gig at East Rutherford's Meadowlands Stadium to mark Bon Jovi Day.

Bon Jovi Day was something of an understatement, for the 1980s

– certainly the latter half – had been Bon Jovi's decade. From September 1986, the band had been living in a dream-cum-nightmare, revelling in phenomenal success yet dragged under by the massive demands on their time and energies. Weary with it all, Jon felt that the time had come for a break, secure in the knowledge that he had done enough work to ensure that the name of Bon Jovi would not be forgotten: 'I would like to think after four albums and a thousand odd shows I could afford to take a year or two off. I'd like to think our fans are familiar enough with our songs so that if in two years time a new Bon Jovi record comes out they'd go "Oh great, I haven't heard them in a while".' As a new decade dawned, it was time to return to a little normality and get a new perspective on life; just as he had in 1980, Jon Bon Jovi wanted to take time to plan the future. Bon Jovi was placed on indefinite hold.

8

HIRED GUN

Much has been made of the responsibility which Doc McGhee and Polygram should bear for working Bon Jovi to the point of collapse during the 1980s, but more especially following the release of *Slippery When Wet*. However, the fault does not lie with them alone, for throughout his twenties Jon Bon Jovi behaved like a man possessed, embracing a manic lifestyle with scarcely a thought for his health or that of the rest of the Bon Jovi troupe.

The seeds of this epic schedule were sown in his childhood love for rock'n'roll. As a bored kid staring out of the window at school, what could possibly be more exciting than playing in a band every night of the week? The bar band ethic was just that – all over Jersey a bunch of groups would be playing the various bars night in, night out. This romantic life beyond accepted society's prim confines was totally absorbing to Jon, who took to it with a vengeance when the opportunity presented itself. Living a rootless existence meant that he could abdicate responsibility for everything in his life except putting on a good show and writing some enjoyable tunes. Once established as a recording act, Jon and the band had a crew and a road manager who would ensure that they didn't have to think about anything but the show; meals, travelling, hotel rooms, entertainment, drink, girls – they were all laid on for them. Although it was a mentally and physically debilitating way to live, going from one town or country to another, it did enable the band to simply cut themselves off from the world outside, shut off their minds and go with the flow. They had no decisions to make for everything was done for them, a typical record company ploy: turn your artists into helpless children and they'll eventually do whatever you tell them because they don't know how else to exist.

There's plenty of evidence, much of it documented earlier in the text, that Jon and the band simply closed down in order to get through the rigours of the five hundred shows that constituted the *Slippery When Wet* and *New Jersey* tours. For one who had been so closely involved in every facet of his early career, better might have been expected of Jon, but in the face of irresistible odds his resolve was ground down and he was transformed into a robot operating on auto pilot except for those two brief hours in the day when he went on stage.

That passion for the stage is another feature of his story and a partial explanation for the way he pushed himself to the very limits of endurance. Jon would be classified as a 'fameophobe' if such a term existed, such is his disdain for the trappings of success. Unlike Madonna or Michael Jackson, Jon had no intention of being ensnared by his celebrity and was almost pathological in his determination to remain an ordinary, decent chap who could go about his business as he pleased, walking the streets at his ease. As a part of his policy of remaining in contact with the grass roots of his following – for good commercial as well as personal reasons – he felt compelled to take energetically to the road. It was only on the concert stage and in the hours around the show that he could meet the people that had put him on his pedestal, that he could tell them and show them that he had not changed and that he could regain his energy and enthusiasm, feeding vampirically on the close, reciprocal relationship he had with them.

To these fine sentiments must be added the lure of filthy lucre. Like anyone born into a working class family, money had never been in great supply during his youth and so its sudden availability in such abundance was naturally enticing and exciting. Having studied his pop music, he also knew full well that – a few select artists apart – there were not too many examples of bands surviving beyond half a dozen years. The urge to make the most of his fifteen minutes of fame, as Warhol defined it, would have been powerful indeed, allowing him to ensure that neither he nor any of his family need ever worry about money again.

Only such a wide range of emotions could explain just why Jon continued to work himself so hard and with such fierce determination. Yet perhaps the greatest single motivating force in his masochist quest to drive himself to the point of clinical exhaustion lay in one facet of his personality: his highly addictive nature. The song 'Stick To Your Guns' from *New Jersey* said a lot about Jon in its lyric, which essentially argues that whatever you do, you should do it to the utmost, believe in it always and never surrender. If Bon Jovi went on tour, Jon had to play more shows than any other band in the world, as his regular boasts insisted. If they were making a record, he had to spend more time working on it in the finest detail, sell more copies than anyone and promote it harder than anyone. Obsessive in the extreme, Jon could become addicted to almost anything that moved him – witness the earlier comments where he craved the applause of the audience. With this in mind, it was fortunate indeed that drugs were never really a feature of the Bon Jovi circle for the consequences might have been dire. Happily, his addictive vices were, in general, rather more wholesome and all played a part in the success of his career.

He could be likened to a child obsessively chewing his way through all the delights in a sweet shop and his addictive nature was in a sense childish, but it was this ability to work towards an objective in a very determined, childlike fashion that ultimately paid dividends. Where more adult, rational minds might have baulked at the size of the odds against Bon Jovi becoming a hit group, Jon simply set his face to the task and got on with it. He simply couldn't get enough of Bon Jovi, being in Bon Jovi and everything that surrounded Bon Jovi. It was this relentless devotion to his belief in himself and his destiny that made his American Dreams into an American reality.

The time came of course when he had had enough of Bon Jovi, when they had done everything they'd dreamt of twice over and were tiring of living in one another's pockets all the year round. So Jon just went back to his original obsession, trading in Bon Jovi for rock'n'roll itself. The *New Jersey* tour finally ended in February

1990, whereupon the five agreed to take a break from one another for a year or so. Richie wanted to do his own solo record, *Stranger In This Town*, David wrote a horror movie soundtrack, *Netherworld*, and Alec and Tico simply took a holiday. The strong bond that had seen them through the madness of the eighties was – if not broken – certainly under severe strain. In July, Jon told *Sounds*, 'Right now there is no desire for me to go back with those four guys and make Bon Jovi this big happy family again. The five of us have not been in one room since the minute we left the dressing room on the way to the stage for the last show of the last tour.' Sensibly realizing that they all required time on their own, time away from Bon Jovi to work out just what it was that had excited them about the band in the first place, the year off was the best solution.

Jon didn't want to get off the treadmill just yet though. His involvement with the *Young Guns II* movie came about almost by accident, but there's little doubt that he would have found something else to occupy his time if that hadn't come along. Indeed he'd already begun another scheme, setting up his own label, Jambco (an acronym for John, Anthony, Matt Bongiovi Company – the real brotherhood). Although he was very keen to sign new artists to the label, in practice little has happened, since Jon's energies have been dissipated elsewhere. In 1990, for instance, he was whisked off to Santa Fe for his acting debut.

Young Guns had been a highly successfuly 'Brat Pack' movie from 1988, featuring Emilio Estevez, Lou Diamond Phillips, Kiefer Sutherland and Charlie Sheen. Given that the western genre had rarely been seen on the movie screen since the boom days of the Sergio Leone/Clint Eastwood spaghetti westerns twenty years earlier, it was only natural that Jon should seek it out assiduously and proclaim it a great film. Once *Young Guns* had fired its way to success, there was no way Hollywood could miss out on a box-office-busting sequel, which again grabbed Jon's attention.

By now a friend to the stars by virtue of the celebrity circus that attended Bon Jovi's every move, Jon had struck up a friendship with Estevez:

We were in the mutual admiration society. In September 1989

he told me they wanted to use 'Wanted Dead or Alive' in *Young Guns II*. He said the writer of *Young Guns* [John Frusco] was inspired to write the movie by 'Wanted'. I was really flattered cos I was such a huge fan of the first movie. In February I said to them, 'it'd be great but you can't use "Wanted". The lyrics don't fit, it's too modern.' So I wrote 'Blaze of Glory' and went to the movie set with that.

Always with an eye for the mythology of the moment, Jon later took to embroidering the story more than somewhat, attempting to turn his involvement with the film into some spur of the moment thing: 'Maybe it's it the Italian in me, but when they invited me down to filming I thought 'I can't turn up empty-handed' so instead of bringing them a bottle of wine I brought them a song.'

However the song sprang up, Jon's musical sensibilities did not let him down, for *Variety* had already commented on the unsuitability of the hard rock score that had accompanied the original movie. While 'Blaze of Glory' leant heavily on the Bon Jovi heritage with its melodramatic chorus, the acoustic instrumentation gave it an archaic flavour wholly appropriate to the time and mood of the film, garnering Jon an Oscar nomination for 'Best Song' along the way. At this stage, it was the only way he was going to bag a nomination, for though *Young Guns II* marked his debut on the silver screen, he made no impression, catching the limelight for just the blink of an eye.

Over many years Jon had always looked down on the idea of going into acting, even though in the pre-Bon Jovi years he had auditioned for a part in *Footloose*. Looking at the long line of rock thespians, it's little wonder that he had such contempt for it, but given his matinée-idol looks, it was no real surprise that the offers kept coming in. Despite the best endeavours of move moguls everywhere, Jon kept out of that particular spotlight and persevered with his music, a choice he has never had any reason to regret. He arrived on the set of *Young Guns II* with no desire to lose his dramatic virginity, but circumstances conspired to force his hand, as he explained in *Sounds*:

I was in Santa Fe with an acoustic guitar and a notebook. I

had to borrow snow gear because it was freezing. I was bored silly ... so I consented to be in the movie – with the writer. The two of us escape from a makeshift jail, I grab the deputy and his gun, we throw the deputy into this jail and as I point the gun, the sheriff blows me away! It takes me longer to explain than to do it!

Escaping with his dignity intact – scarcely anyone actually noticed him in the film itself – Jon was nevertheless inspired by his time on the set, his proximity to the world of cinema and also by the story that they were telling. During the course of his stay he read through the screenplay and that, together with a screening of a rough cut of the film, reawakened the songwriting fire in him. He drew inspiration from earlier westerns that had made an impression on him, most notably one which had featured Bob Dylan in one of his mercifully-rare acting performances. Looking back on the sound-track that had accompanied that film, Jon found that he was able to create an atmosphere that worked successfully for him and his songs: 'When I saw the Sam Peckinpah versions of *Pat Garrett And Billy The Kid*, I realised Dylan not only had 'Knockin' On Heaven's Door' but two or three other songs in there. So one song turned into two, four turned into eight, I saw a rough cut of the movie and wrote another two and made it an even ten.' Within a matter of days he had penned sufficient material to cover the entire film sound-track, though since they were all songs rather than instrumental pieces, much of his work was too obtrusive and remained unused in the final cut.

Despite this particular set-back, Jon was understandably taken with the simpler feel he'd been able to capture in his songwriting and felt that he ought to record the music he had. Taking advantage of the mutually agreed hiatus, he began to assemble a loose alliance of musicians that might do justice to these new and stylistically rather different songs. He expended considerable thought on the arrangements and concluded that 'I had to go back to real basics – acoustic guitar, accordion, harmonica'. To achieve this requisite mood, he enlisted the help of Aldo Nova, a guitarist whom he had signed to the Jambco label and who had contributed to the *Bon Jovi* album. There was no suggestion, however, that electric guitars would be completely ignored purely for historical authenticity.

If Jon and Nova made up the backbone of the group that would work on this *Young Guns II* project, additional musicians would obviously prove necessary. Revelling in the kudos that his fame and reputation brought with them, Jon called up such rock'n'roll luminaries as Jeff Beck, Elton John and Little Richard to add their own distinctive stamp to the proceedings, while Kenny Aronoff added drums and Benmont Tench from Tom Petty's Heartbreakers flavoured the music with some telling keyboard work.

Naturally enough, the central song itself was 'Blaze of Glory', Jon's first song for the film. Opening on acoustic guitar and rising to a crescendo with Beck's guitar solo, the song was a nice example of his writing style in microcosm: a gentle start building slowly to an all-consuming chorus built around a memorable hook. There were several examples of this kind of song on the album, which suffered if anything from a lack of variety; required to write an entire album without any assistance, Jon fell back on his old standbys in much the same way that Richie did on his solo album. If nothing else, their respective records indicated that together they had a chemistry that gave results which exceeded the sum of the constituent parts.

Even so *Blaze of Glory,* as the album came to be known, was impressive fare, as Barry McIlheney wrote in *Q*: 'A rewarding insight into the solo preoccupations of the Jesse James of rock'. Even a critic as previously antipathetic towards Bon Jovi as Adam Sweeting was forced to concede in the *Guardian* that 'The cowboy theme obviously fits him like a glove. Jon Bon Jovi's rockist fantasies sometimes go way overboard but God, can he write a hook. The question is does Jon Bon Jovi need his band any more?' In pure commercial terms the answer was a resounding 'no', for he sold more than two million copies of the album in America alone as it reached number three, the title-track single with its widescreen MTV-friendly video hitting the number one slot. By this stage though Jon was coming to realize that not everything of value in his musical life could be measured by chart positions alone.

The solo experience left Jon missing his compatriots in Bon Jovi, as indeed it had been designed to do, but he remained steadfast in his determination not to call on his erstwhile colleagues for any assistance on the project, however strong the temptation might have been.

> I was listening to some live tapes cos in the meantime we're working on a live album ... and I was so close to picking up the phone and going 'C'mon Tico'. But I just didn't wanna do it with the band ... I was having a blast, I've been with the band eight years, more than I've been with my brother or my wife. I know what those guys do in the day and the night and how they sleep and eat.

Absence made the heart grow fonder and Jon was determined that time should run its course, rekindling their enthusiasm for working with one another.

He came out of *Blaze of Glory* with credit and he could be proud of what he achieved on the album. Much of the material stood up well alongside the music that Bon Jovi had made as a band. The relaxed manner in which it had been compiled was an invigorating experience too in the light of the pressure under which *New Jersey* had been recorded. Continuing the process of musical education that he had begun a decade or more earlier, Jon was keen to see how legendary figures such as Beck or Elton John worked in the studio and was intrigued by the professional manner in which they carried themselves, playing their parts without fuss and then moving on to something else. There was nothing of the frenetic atmosphere that had clouded his recent days with the band and it was an attitude that he determined to take with him into the future.

He reflected on this change in *Sounds*, where he was adamant about the album's genesis and its future: 'This absolutely and positively is not a solo album. I don't want anybody misconstruing it as that or as the next Bon Jovi record. This is art for the sake of art. I don't think this album would be right for the band.' Though laying himself open to charges of pretension when calling his record 'art', it was an honest assessment of the way in which he had tackled the project. There was no possibility of touring the material, no desire to flog it around the world to sell another million copies, just a compulsion to make some music that interested, entertained, amused and moved him, and put it on record so that other like-minded individuals could buy it if they wanted it.

This was significant indeed for it marked the first signs that Jon was waking from the nightmare that he had been locked into since *Slippery When Wet* turned into a global phenomenon. It also spelled the end for Doc McGhee, for at last Jon had begun to comprehend just what had been at the root of his mindless workload of the previous few years; it had not been his workaholic nature alone, but the demands of what could only be described as a slave-driving managerial philosophy. Those days were gone for good.

Every song on *Blaze of Glory* was directly related to a scene from the film, but there were times when he appeared to be writing as much about himself as the events up on the screen. In 'Billy Get Your Guns' for instance, he wrote about the price that having a reputation demands. In cinematic terms for the purposes of *Young Guns II*, being the fastest gun in the west only increases the price on your head and brings your impending demise ever closer. In the record industry, Jon had to accept that there was always some new kid on the block that wanted to take over his mantle as the world's biggest rock star. In the aftermath of *New Jersey*, W. Axl Rose and Guns'N'Roses had come in search of Bon Jovi's throne and taken it from them. This addiction to staying in the number one slot was just another contributory factor in deciding the nature of Jon's workload; those at the top are often the ones who work harder and longer than anyone else. 'Billy Get Your Guns' was yet another signal that he was beginning to discover the attendant disadvantages of fame and fortune. Reflecting on his own past and on the media coverage of every facet of Axl Rose's life, he admitted, 'I don't envy [him] the spotlight. I'm not afraid of . . . anything, just the constant scrutiny.'

If he was in a personal state of flux, there were certain constants that remained rock solid within his writing, such as the devotion to friends and the ideal of loyalty. That was addressed in 'Blood Money', one of the most striking songs on the album. It was arranged specifically so that the consequences of betrayal were made crystal clear: 'I left a three second gap of silence before the next song. I wanted it to sink in. I faded it purposely so that the last word you hear is 'Grave' ... it was written for a specific scene where the law bought Garrett. For a thousand dollars he turned into Judas and stabbed his best friend.'

And where would a rock'n'roll outlaw be if it weren't for Phil Lynott? Homage was duly paid on 'Never Say Die' which was 'influenced' shall we say by Lynott's anthem 'The Boys Are Back In Town'. Jon had no alternative but to come clean: 'That three chord intro does remind me of Thin Lizzy. Phil certainly did write some great cowboy songs.' How subconscious this influence was is hard to say, but it was perhaps no coincidence that a couple of years earlier Bon Jovi had recorded the Thin Lizzy song for the Make A Difference Foundation album *Stairway To Heaven/Highway To Hell*, a rather dodgy concept record which featured various artists covering the songs of those who had died through alcohol or drug abuse.

If Jon had lost some of his interest in the music business, *Blaze of Glory* helped him to recapture it, so much so that in the summer of 1990 he was back on the road again, this time as part of a back-to-the-roots exercise, playing rhythm guitar with Southside Johnny and The Asbury Jukes:

We played bars, I had a room-mate for the first time in my career ... we drove around in a van, stayed in Quality Inns, no wardrobe girls, no crew, you loaded your own gear. It was pretty rough but it was great. The last show we played was in Asbury. That was cool. In Asbury with your hero and I'm just playing rhythm guitar and singing a little harmony.

Going full circle back to the Jersey bars that had nurtured him a decade and more earlier, Jon seemed to be enjoying the break from Bon Jovi. Certainly there were no immediate plans to get back together in the autumn of 1990, as he confirmed with a hint of self-sufficient arrogance: 'These are my best friends, brothers ... in time we'll put it back together ... when I make Bon Jovi records they're essentially my records anyhow.'

132

Plans to release a live Bon Jovi record were indefinitely shelved for fear of saturating the market place, as he told *Select*: 'The idea was that we'd go away for a couple of years, give everyone a break. Yet what with one project or another, it seems as if we're drowning the market rather than leaving it alone! I'm a workaholic and I'll never slow down.' That last statement barely out of his mouth, he found that he had reached the end of his rope: 'The burn-out set in and the withdrawals began, I was learning to become a human being again.'

9

A LEAP OF FAITH

The complete physical and mental exhaustion that racked Jon towards the end of 1990 and on into 1991 would hardly have been any great surprise to those who had observed the amount of work that he had undertaken. Reading contemporary interviews and looking at pictures of him on and off stage, it's clear that behind the fixed smile and glazed expression of the showbiz trooper, there was a wreck trying to crawl out. Yet all the while he was looking to deny its existence. As the *New Jersey* tour came to a conclusion, Bon Jovi were booked to play a string of lucrative dates at London's Wembley Arena immediately after Christmas 1989, having finished a German tour on December 23rd – all of which meant that they could not return home for the festivities.

At the time, Jon claimed this to be some sort of triumph for the rock'n'roll lifestyle, excitedly telling the world how he and his tribe didn't need the rest of the world: 'I got the band and the crew and the road manager and a coupla other people and y'know we're spending Christmas together in a hotel!' Once he had rediscovered the use of all his mental faculties a few years later, he described it as 'rotten', pointedly remarking that his agents, lawyers, record company executives and personal manager had all returned to their respective homes.

This particular incident was not an isolated case of the band being exploited while others enjoyed the spoils, but a symptom of a wider sickness. As has already been documented elsewhere, industry and managerial wisdom dictated that, just in case Bon Jovi weren't a band that could go on indefinitely, it was best to milk them for every penny while their popularity endured. The money-men were fortunate that in Jon they had a man who believed very strongly in both the importance of his audience and in the work ethic and who was prepared to go along with tour after tour in the misguided belief that he was living out his dreams and keeping in touch with the source of his popularity.

Jon wasn't the only member of the band to feel his exertions sapping his energy of course, but as the frontman the pressures on him were more intense. Everyone wanted to talk to him rather than Alec or Tico so he had to do the interviews. The band carried his name and so if the shows weren't up to scratch, he would carry the can; therefore he had to put extra time into ensuring that the production values were sufficient to wow the crowds. Finally, as the singer his performance was far more physically demanding than those of the others. He had to cover every inch of stage, he had to sing at the top of his voice, he had to reach out to every member of the audience, all the while knowing that everything depended on him. If Alec had an off night, few would notice, nor would they care; if Jon's voice let him down or if he couldn't put on the effervescent display expected of him, the whole evening collapsed. Ticket holders would be disappointed, the critics unforgiving.

His respect for his audience was such that he maintained the punishing pace at a considerable risk to his own health: 'Doctors gave me massive steroid jabs to keep me going and take the swelling off my vocal chords'. Initially the scars on his throat were worn as a bade of masculine pride, the machismo aspect of working through his pain undeniably appealing to him. Even through his self-delusion, Jon knew that a day of reckoning would eventually have to come. The physical manifestations of a mental malaise were increasingly frightening:

I couldn't get in a lift without breaking into a sweat . . . [the *New Jersey* tour] left me crawling the walls with exhaustion and the strain of the shows left me thinking I was half mad. I'd convince myself I was okay but then I'd look in the mirror, see a grey face with big black circles round the eyes and not recognize who I was.

Jon was not alone, for other members of the entourage had their encounters with various unhealthy palliatives to see them through to the other end of the long dark touring tunnel. Inevitably, as their individual health began to fail, so the relationships that existed between them fell prey to exhaustion, reaching the point at which they effectively suffered a communal nervous breakdown. Jon told *Hot Press* that 'the whole phase of our career got pretty heavy towards the end but at least we learnt from the experience. To tell you the truth there's nothing that can happen any more that I haven't already seen.'

Useful knowledge for future work, but the overwhelming requirement by February 1990 was to take time off – a vacation that had recharged everyone's batteries by the time they regrouped for further work almost two years later. Things were not as simple as that bald statement implies, however. As the previous chapter illustrated, Jon did not come off the road, put his feet up and spend a year resting and recuperating. His hyperactive nature, along with the opportunities which presented themselves to him, ensured that no sooner was he back home with his new wife than he was off on his travels again, storing up more exhaustion.

The central motif of Jon's life has been his urge to run away – to run away from the nine-to-five, to run away from responsibility, to run away from relationships. With the benefit of hindsight, it's pretty obvious that the work he undertook through 1990 on *Young Guns II* and with Southside Johnny was simply a ploy to help him avoid going back to his new home, putting down roots and living a life as the head of his family. All of this implied growing up, putting the life he had lived and loved since he was a teenager behind him. Given his compulsive personality and his behaviour in the past, it's likely that he viewed it as an all-or-nothing situation. If he became domesticated, he could no longer be a rock'n'roller, and vice versa. He maintained his momentum until March 1991, at which point he finally got some time off and simply ground to a halt:

What I really needed was a complete break . . . it kinda creeps up on you and there's only one solution, you have to pull the plug and get off the road. The simplest things made me fly off the handle. I was in such a weird mood that people couldn't be normal around me, even my closest family. Everybody was treading carefully in case they triggered me off.

That a man who puts such a high price on loyalty and dedication to friends and family should have allowed himself to get into such a state says much about the seductive sedative that is the cosseted rock'n'roll lifestyle he was used to living – how comfortable it was to be inured from the horrors of the outside world and how difficult it was for an addictive type such as Jon to give that up. It also speaks volumes for the fear that he had of 'normality' for he was clearly willing to go to any lengths to avoid it.

What were the reasons for this fear? He had apparently sorted out a relatively stable relationship with Dorothea, his wife since April 1989. His wildest days of excess on the road seemed to be behind him and he was materially secure for life. All that he required was the opportunity to relax for a few months, get back into shape and then resume his career. Why flee from that? Again we have to go back to his intransigent response to the idea of growing up. He had intimated in the course of the *New Jersey* interviews that he was gradually coming to terms with the concept but still seemed less than eager to go the whole hog and throw himself into adulthood. As something of a gypsy, the assumption has to be that he enjoyed travelling – yet the problem went deeper than the removal of his hobby. As an addictive personality and a compulsive over-achiever in pursuit of that American Dream he had held so dear, Jon may only have felt alive in front of a crowd. Certainly his role as a musician gave his existence a validity that it might not otherwise have had; a year away from his career may have left him looking into a gaping hole.

Subconsciously, perhaps he felt that married life would stifle him, cramp his style and drain inspiration from him as a songwriter. Cosy domesticity has certainly drawn the fire from numerous writers in the past, yet Jon had never been an angry or aggressive artist. Settling down to life at his new home could scarcely make a difference to his musical output. No, it seems that in going home he realized he was crossing his personal Rubicon, moving on to mature responsibility, and it was something that he found hard to face. He admitted to being confused and depressed for much of the time at the prospect of this new scenario, emotions that were only exacerbated by his state of near physical collapse. Consequently the two conditions fed off one another. He explained, 'I was sitting there in a fog, I was questioning my professional and personal life, a lot of emotions pulling me different ways.'

There's a strong case to be made that Jon was finally going through his adolescent identity crisis fifteen years late. Having put his emotions, if not his hormones, on hold when he was a teenager, everything else subordinated to his overweening ambition, he was finally having to come to terms with who he was and what he was doing with his life: 'I was in a mess. I'd been sitting in my house with some friends saying "what's it all about?"' He tried psychiatric help at this stage though that was quickly shelved when he realized that like everyone else, his therapist worked to the clock, meting out exactly the amount of treatment that had been paid for and no more, leaving him in a terrible state at the end of the session with nowhere else to go.

Eventually, Jon was to answer his own questions as to just what had gone so terribly wrong to leave him feeling so depressed, but in the interim life was not pleasant for him or those around him. 'It was only when we finally came off the road that we went to pieces,' he said later. When he finally went home in March '91, 'It took me two weeks to unpack my suitcase because I couldn't face being at home. Dorothea kept trying to take my clothes out of the case and I'd scream at her to leave them.' While he was trying to pull himself together and sort out his own mental state, further problems were caused by the media.

At this time, Jon required all his energy to concentrate on his personal life, but he wasn't given leave for that. With Bon Jovi now out of sight for over a year, the press began to run stories that the band had split up, adding spurious quotes that suggested irrevocable rifts between the members of the band, especially Jon and Richie. Richie supposedly did not like the financial arrangements in the group, Jon allegedly said that Richie's liaison with Cher had gone to his head and was upsetting the group equilibrium. With an air of resignation in his voice, Jon told *Q*, 'the English press is so powerful because that shit goes world fucking wide ... it caused a lot of tension in the band ... it starts shit up between you.' Warming to his theme elsewhere, he added, 'the band always prided itself on never fighting each other. We went on vacations together, we lived together ... but we're all believing the press.'

That tension was released over Christmas 1990 when they reconvened to play a brief tour of Japan, Jon issuing the stark warning that 'if it's fun then next Spring we'll start writing and if not I'm going to cool it and pursue a solo career'. Yet the *Young Guns II* experience had made it abundantly clear to him that a solo career was not what he really wanted out of life: 'It took playing with other people to realise how much I liked playing with my guys ... if I left the band and had a great solo career or a shitty solo career, no matter what I did, I wouldn't be doing it for the first time. We headlined Donington, we achieved a dream together.' The history they shared and the genuine camaraderie that had pulled them through the difficult early years when the Bon Jovi career was stuttering along were foremost in Jon's mind as he looked to his future.

Had he ever felt the need, he could have easily pulled the plug on Bon Jovi. After all, it was his name on the records, he was the principal songwriter and it was his face as much as anyone's that sold the concert tickets. The success of *Blaze of Glory* had illustrated that he had a perfectly viable solo career ready and waiting for him should he choose to follow it, with the added attraction that any musicians involved would very obviously be hired hands rather than the quasi-band members that he'd begun Bon Jovi with. On his own he could call the shots without any concern for the finer feelings of his musicians. But that was not his way. Although he was the group's figurehead and although he liked to ensure that things were done according to his wishes, he genuinely enjoyed the band spirit, the atmosphere those five people created when they went into the studio together. Unless the

Japanese shows proved to be an absolute disaster, he was convinced that Bon Jovi would and should continue.

To reinforce the point, he told another story about his experiences on the set of *Young Guns II*: 'I stated hanging out on the set ... the actors were very friendly but when filming was over they said goodbye and went off alone. It made me glad I was in a band and I missed the others. There are 50,000 singers and as many songwriters better than me but when we're all together it's magic.' That view had been strengthened in November 1990 when the group were presented with the Silver Clef Award at the Nordoff-Robbins Therapy Centre lunch, recognition for their contribution to popular music. The charity aspect of the award was welcome too – Nordoff-Robbins use music as part of their therapy programme for disabled children – for that was a line that Bon Jovi were increasingly involved in. Just prior to Christmas 1990 and the shows in the Far East, the group reassembled for the first of what became an annual event – a benefit show in New Jersey.

The concerts proved to be just the kind of catharsis they required; while they accepted they still had their disagreements, the air was cleared and the gigs were fun. Other commitments meant that they could not get down to work straight away – Richie was working on his own album and readying himself for a solo tour, for instance – and so they left one another with an agreement that they would meet up later in the year to thrash out their differences and, hopefully, get back to work.

It was during this limbo period that Jon had the personal problems mentioned earlier, so it is perfectly reasonable to suggest that the future was still less than assured for Bon Jovi. They had all agreed to meet up in October 1991. Using a record company house, they ensured that only the five of them would be present at a gathering that would decide once and for all whether or not Bon Jovi would be able to continue. Jon sat down at the table with a mixed hand; the others in the band had been right in insisting that Bon Jovi should take a break for the good of their collective health, even if at the time he had questioned their loyalty to the cause. Jon had been the inspiration for their rise to pre-eminence and had now carved out a solo niche for himself, so that in commercial terms he had no further need for the band identity, balancing out any debt he might have owed them for taking care of his physical state. It was with this in mind that he came to the most important session of the group's career.

'We had a make or break weekend in a house on a Caribbean island. I warned my wife that I might be back in a couple of days. I had a dozen songs I wanted to play to the guys. They didn't want to hear them. Instead we learnt how to be a band again. We had a few beers and remembered what we were in it for.' To the great relief of all concerned, Bon Jovi were back in business and ready to attack a new decade. With Richie about to embark on a brief solo tour, they agreed to take a couple of months away from one another and reconvene for work on the new album in January 1992, although they did play a charity show in Jersey again just before Christmas.

It appears that despite all the bickering, all the media invention and all the squabbles, deep down the five were never in any doubt that Bon Jovi should carry on into the 1990s. The less charitable might not be surprised at this, suggesting that throwing away Bon Jovi would be like throwing away a blank cheque, and there's more than a grain of truth in that assessment – but there was more to it than that. In the days before Bon Jovi the band became Bon Jovi Inc., multinational conglomerate and money-making machine, there was a genuine empathy between the five of them. The station wagon days of criss-crossing America had been exciting, they had many memories to share over a beer in the evenings and musically they were still perfectly attuned to each other. To allow Bon Jovi to go down without a fight would have been a sad way to see it all end.

Once the decision to continue had been made, you might have thought that everything would be plain sailing. All the infrastructure was in place, the record company was looking forward to their album, they could write and record wherever they wanted. All the omens were good and since they hadn't recorded together in three and a half years, surely they would approach the new sessions with verve and vigour, giving the group a new lease of energetic life. They were undoubtedly looking forward to the challenge of working together again, and yet a week or so into rehearsals Jon found that he was 'sitting in my basement, wondering why we weren't excited to be together. It was because we were afraid it would just pick up where we left off – exhaustion, tension, the machine. Then we realised that firing everybody was the way to go.' In public the decision was justified on the grounds that Doc had diversified too far and had too many other acts on his books, but in reality other factors were far more significant.

The terrors of the previous years had made an indelible mark on them all, a far deeper wound than any cared to admit. If Jon had shown the most obvious scars from the trials they had gone through, everyone had been affected in some way and all were terrified of having to go through the same ordeal again. The solution was simple and apparently effective, for once they had sacked their back-room staff and released the weight of their expectations from their shoulders, writing and recording progressed smoothly.

Doc McGhee has often been cast as the villain of the piece throughout this narrative. His pre-Bon Jovi drug-dealing days are totally indefensible, but then so is much of his handling of his charges. In regular contact with the band he must have seen the signs of fatigue and breakdown that they were displaying so obviously on the road, must have realized that he was pushing them too hard, and yet deliberately chose to ignore the evidence in order to ensure that the revenue kept flowing into the Bon Jovi account.

There are two sides to every story though, and while Doc could be castigated for his uncaring attitude towards Jon and the others, you must also look at his record of success. He was an important character in Bon Jovi's rise to the top. He made the best deals, organized wonderful promotional opportunities and ensured that they were rarely out of the news. When coupled with the effortlessly commercial songs that Jon and Richie were churning out, it proved to be an irresistible force that carried all before it. As an individual, Doc clearly had a number of faults, yet as a manger few could have been as dedicated to the cause of his clients as he was, even at the risk of alienating other artists that he represented; remember the way in which he made Bon Jovi the very obvious headliners in Moscow and the financially advantageous arrangements that Jon had with Skid Row? From that point of view, Jon could not have had a more astute adviser and he does owe Doc a debt of gratitude.

That debt was of course discharged in full when Bon Jovi embarked on the suicidal schedule that Doc booked for them. If the tours and the records were making Jon a very rich man, they were just as beneficial to Doc. He had the added advantage of being able to stay at home while the band were on the road, enjoying the chance to watch the bank balance go up and up. The agreement between Bon Jovi and Doc McGhee was, in the end, mutually beneficial but it was a partnership that had run its course long before it was put to rest.

Jon took some flak for this decision, some arguing that it went against his oath of loyalty. Yet this was a fallacious claim for, if anything, it had been Doc that had abused Jon's commitment; he had manipulated a number of events – most notably the Make A Difference show in Moscow – for his own ends and could have been accused of using Bon Jovi to further his own career. Certainly his very high profile position within the organization made it especially easy for him to find other clients. All of this might have been forgivable as examples of the ordinary, if seedy, way in which the wheels of commerce turn. What Bon Jovi could not forget was the heinous crime that he had perpetrated when he worked them to the point of disintegration from 1986 to the beginning of 1990. Not only had he threatened their health with his insatiable desire to chase another few thousand dollars wherever it could be had, he had put the very future of the band at risk. That was unforgivable and it was that that finished him with Bon Jovi. At the end of their relationship and with the aid of a crystal ball, a few questions and answers spell out the impact on each of their time together and how all parties benefited to some degree:

Would Bon Jovi had been successful without Doc? Yes.

Would they have been so successful? Probably not.

Would they have come so close to splitting up? No.

Would they have been healthier people? Yes.

Would they have made better records? It's very likely.

Would Doc have achieved success without Bon Jovi? Yes.

The entire Bon Jovi organisation was overhauled and streamlined to ensure that the key decisions were taken, nominally by the group themselves, though in practice Jon generally had the final say. This was true about the recording of their fifth album, *Keep The Faith*, which was put together with Bob Rock at the helm back in Vancouver's Little Mountain Studios, over the course of six months, the longest period the band had ever spent on recording. This was indicative of the importance with which Jon in particular was approaching this new project.

Many, many things had changed since *New Jersey* had been written and recorded, both on a personal and a global level. Music itself had been irreversibly changed; everything had been up for grabs and a number of groups had taken advantage. Over the course of that period artists such as Nirvana, Pearl Jam and Guns N' Roses transformed the commercial end of the hard rock genre, while the likes of Extreme were able completely to alter everyone's conception of what mainstream rock could be by making themselves acceptable to a wider range of people than even the Doc-inspired Bon Jovi had ever dreamt of.

Jon responded to the challenge by redefining what he felt Bon Jovi should be. They had rarely descended to the bathetic level of Bryan Adams nor had they ever been as raw as Nirvana, especially when they were recording for the Sub Pop label. The obvious course, that which would have been advised by accountants and executives, would have been to steer a middle course between the two, yet Jon was now far more culturally ambitious than he had ever been before. His time away from the industry had sharpened his musical instincts so that it was the songs that were paramount in his mind, not the financial rewards which he no longer had to chase. He admitted with a degree of remorse that 'in that time we were off the road I really learned that there was a difference between having a great song and a hit song . . . now I don't really care if I never write another hit song again. It's more important to grow as a writer than capitalise on previous successes.'

A skilful repositioning of Bon Jovi as a credible modern unit for the 1990s had its positive side, but it was an enterprise fraught with danger. Through the eighties, in spite of the massive popularity they had enjoyed, critics had thrown brickbats at this collection of bimboys whom they accused of a wanton lack of depth or originality and who were apparently coasting to success on the strength of their loks. It was a charge that held an element of truth, for Jon's statements on politics and the environment showed an appalling lack of knowledge about the dangers facing the world; his avowed preference for the hedonistic delights of seeking out a good time wherever and whenever it was to be had rather than giving any thought to life, the universe and everything may have sounded fine in the midst of the Yuppie boom, but as the *New Jersey* tour came to an end, it seemed shallow and selfish.

By 1992, Jon was big enough to hold up his hands and admit his culpability: 'I guess you could say that doing this album was like waking from a dream' he admitted when challenged about the change in his lyrical direction. Considering his failings, he accepted that the time spent in the air-conditioned bubble of success was time that might have been better used looking outside rather than within:

The *Young Guns II* sound-track kept me in the spotlight for another year. I didn't get time off until March '91. Then I just laid back and looked around me. I couldn't have written *Keep The Faith* a second earlier, if I hadn't had time to see the 'cardboard condos' in New York City and what twelve years of Reaganomics has done to this country.

Needless to say, in 1992 he voted for Bill Clinton, but the evidence of American decay had been there in 1989 when he had said of George Bush 'he's cool. I like George.' By 1992, the word was 'vote for Bill because George Bush [is] just too out of touch with the human race.'

Unfortunately Jon had not had the eyes to see the damage wrought on his country until years later, as he admitted in the song 'Save A Prayer', which caught him in a mood of helpless hopelessness, his blank, fazed vocal telling the tale of a nation living a lie. His opinions had been challenged and swiftly changed by events such as the Los Angeles riots: 'Maybe I was naïve but I never imagined the L.A. riots happening and you know, that hit me hard.'

With the fervour of the converted, he then saw Jambco as an outlet for the voice of protest and he admitted to *Hot Press* that 'I'd love to unearth a budding Ice-T because I think the rap community's saying what the whole of America – and certain sections of white society especially – should be listening to.'

His greatest problem in embracing this new agenda was his celebrated past that had extolled the virtues of much of what he was now standing against. Relying on his accumulated business acumen to see him through, he felt, perfectly correctly, that the Bon Jovi image required a little work. Anton Corbijn was engaged to arrange the transformation. Inevitably he proved to be the perfect choice; the premier photographer working in popular music, Corbijn is best known for his epochal pictures of U2 in the desert for *The Joshua Tree* sleeve. His grainy, monochrome shots almost automatically confer an air of *gravitas* and substance on a band, and the cover and publicity photographs that accompanied *Keep The Faith* helped Jon on the way towards the new image that he coveted. For himself, he had removed the poodle-inspired locks of the past and opted for a shorter cut which conspired to move him still further from the image of extended adolescence which had served him so well.

Imagery and presentation are vital components of the musical mix for any major league artist, but without good songs any success is doomed to be transient. For *Keep The Faith*, Jon was determined that the Bon Jovi reinvention should succeed and so he and Richie approached their songwriting with greater care than ever before. Realizing that he would only have one shot at musical realignment, Jon understood the stakes for which he was playing. If *Keep The Faith* failed, not only would he have failed to attain the credibility he now demanded but he would risk alienating the core Bon Jovi audience too. Forced into the same kind of balancing act that had characterized *New Jersey*, he was more adventurous on this occasion, cautious crowd-pleasing moments reduced to a minimum.

The central song on the album was 'Dry County', a mini-road movie, a travelogue that reflected on the American nation in decline, an indictment of the Reagan/Bush years. Far more than a simple political polemic, 'Dry County' saw Jon digging among his own roots, applying his working class experience to a tale of a boom town gone bust, the reflective guitar and piano accompaniment catching his sombre mood nicely. This was a story of real people facing real hardship, struggling to make ends meet, to bring some meaning into their lives beyond the fight against starvation. The use of religious imagery at the beginning of the track also brought his anger with the organized church to the fore once again as he railed against their detached impotence in the face of very real human need.

That song – like much of the record's attitude – was born from a seminal experience in Jon's life. Still suffering from the after effects of his years of touring, he and some friends chose to ride across America on their Harleys: 'Dorothea planned out the routes and how many miles we should cover each day ... it was a great opportunity to take time out together and remember what it was like without everyone waiting on us ... I just looked back on what I did and saw what I liked and didn't like about it.' Not only did the journey give him time to think things through and sort out his own life, it forced him to look at the country around him, exposing him to the ordinary people that he hadn't seen in a decade. More than any news reports, this brought home to him the reality of economic deprivation and the squalor in which so many of his countrymen and women were forced to live. In the same vein, on the *Keep The Faith* tour Jon sanctioned Red Cross collections for victims of the US floods, people whose lives had been wrecked by an act of God rather than economic mismanagement. Jon's reaction was one of simple compassion: 'It really made an impression on me to realize that people's homes are gone, their crops are gone, their lives are gone and this is the middle of America.'

The title track was born out of this same feeling of desperation and is inextricably linked with 'Dry County', though it went far deeper. Superficially at least, it was propelled by a burning anger at the injustices of society, the hard times that were being rained down on those that could not protect themselves. Sonically highly modern and incorporating the extremely fashionable shuffle beat, it was an inventive departure for the group. At its core was a note of apology, presumably directed towards his wife, for his wayward lifestyle of the past. A defiant rejection of what had gone before, 'Keep The Faith' was a promise to hold on to the good things in life, as he accepted later: 'I took a real chance ... nobody expected me to have a socially conscious song and to be apologising for the things I'd done in my past.'

Yet *Keep The Faith* was not the clearing house it might have been. Commenting on the grunge explosion and the trend-based music industry in general, Jon argued that he had to be true to himself: laudable sentiments. Almost in the same breath though, he argued that the album was a departure from what had gone before, that Bon Jovi were a viable rock act for the 1990s. *Keep The Faith* was not the profound reinvention that Jon would have had the world believe and it's nonsense to suggest that it was or could have been. A little wiser and more worldly perhaps, essentially he remained the same Jon Bon Jovi that had worked on *New Jersey* and *Slippery When Wet*.

This is clear from a cursory listen to some of the Bon Jovi standards that litter the album. 'I'll Sleep When I'm Dead' may well have been a tongue-in-cheek portrayal of the legendary life of a touring band from an older man's perspective but it was still mindless, good time pop. Nothing wrong in that, it's true, but you can't pass old-fashioned guitar boogie off as a radical new direction for rock'n'roll. 'Woman In Love' was similarly traditional fare, a kind of metallic Beach Boys feel that was girls, girls, girls all the way. Songs such as these were hard to understand alongside the maturity of 'Dry County' or 'Keep The Faith', except as a sop to the long-term fans of the group.

It was this assiduous concern for their fanbase that, once again, stopped Bon Jovi in their tracks, for *Keep The Faith* as an album could have gone so much further than it did and Jon might have redefined his position in the rock world in one fell swoop. An example of his innately conservative personality, a nature encouraged by the antediluvian attitudes of the hard rock fraternity, came when he dropped a remix of 'Keep The Faith'. As he explained later, 'We got Mike Edwards of Jesus Jones to do the remix but we ended up deciding not to release it. Edwards did a fine job but it's not time for an acid Bon Jovi.' But why not? It was this trepidation that ultimately left *Keep The Faith* a flawed creation. When contemporaries such as U2 and INXS felt that the time was right to update their musical vocabulary, they did not baulk at employing the remixers. Admittedly they were not always entirely successful experiments but it gave notice that here were bands willing to tamper with their public image, adventurous artists trying to push back their own frontiers. The effect of such a remix is not necessarily in the result itself but in the psychological impact of taking a chance, allowing for a reappraisal by those beyond the cosy confines of the band's hard core following.

'Fear' was a case in point. It opened with the kind of chaotic sampled sound collage that was de rigeur at the time, but where U2 had layered sample upon sample to create a wholly disorientating buzz, Bon Jovi were apologetic, mannered, polite. Taking up the contemporary theme of people anaesthetized to the plight of the real world – and here Jon must have been thinking of his own conduct in the past – the modern hard rock idiom that the band were working in was suitably impressive but not sufficiently challenging. Jon's social commentary and his anti-politician rant were exciting evidence that he was waking from a dream, waking indeed from the American Dream that he had been living; the man who made a career from being a runaway was now declaring that he was ready to stand and fight for what was right. But such a personal revolution deserved a musical revolution too. That is not to say that 'Fear' wasn't a good song – it was very good – just that it could have been so much more had it not foundered on the rocks of his musical reticence.

Few could deny Jon's new-found commitment to the ideal of greater social awareness or justice, but the application of his principles needed work. For instance, while decrying the years of Reaganomics, he did not make any comment on the highly advantageous personal taxation system from which he had benefited during *Slippery When Wet*. Under a different administration, he would have found his income severely reduced by taxes; under Reagan and then Bush, he was able to keep a far higher proportion of his earnings. This reduction in the tax rate at the top end meant less government money could be channelled into social programmes. It also meant that the lower and middle income earners were bearing a disproportionate amount of the tax raising burden.

Such were the contradictory signs coming from the newly politicized Jon Bon Jovi that while it was clear where he stood, it was less easy to discern whether or not he understood the implications. 'Guilt about having money? No' he replied when questioned about the morality of his great wealth. 'Every day I ask "Why have I been so lucky?" but I don't feel guilty about it . . . we finance local charities like a hostel for battered women and a food bank. You see poverty all the time. Well, welcome to America. The album is about making an effort to change that.'

Keep The Faith was, partially at least, about transforming the culture into a more equitable and caring society. His current creed was spelled out in the album opener 'I Believe'. The Queen-influenced intro subsidised into a platitudinous display of emotion, but slowly Jon wrested control of the clichés and turned them into a wider manifesto, looking contemptuously on a world of oppression and by virtue of a very powerful vocal performance, arguing for a belief in the light, urging his audience to stand up for themselves and demand a better world. Some dismissed it as trite, but his anti-cynicism argument was little different from U2's lyrical thrust which was widely approved; clearly the image overhaul hadn't fully worked the miracle. The theme was reprised in the optimistic wash of 'Little Bit Of Soul', which was musically noteworthy for its appropriation of a Rolling Stones feel.

In fact the Stones were the main musical influence on the record, with 'I Want You' having similarities to 'Angie' and 'Blame It On The Love Of Rock'n'Roll' bearing more than a passing resemblance to 'Honky Tonk Women'. A bluesy standard, the latter seemed autobiographical and completely unrepentant in tone; Jon was not sorry for having grown up to be a rock'n'roller and was not disowning his earlier work. All that was happening was that he was growing older and as he matured he became increasingly concerned with the world as a whole rather than Bon Jovi's world.

Outside these strident attacks, *Keep The Faith* retained its fair share of love songs, though even here there were quirks at work. 'If

I Was Your Mother' lived up to the bizarre title with its Beatlesque strings juxtaposed against a metallic guitar to good effect, the themes of dislocation and despair offering greater potential than the simple love songs he'd offered earlier. His musings on the darker side of love extended to 'I Want You', which also touched on ideas that 'Keep The Faith' had first uncovered. It was an apologia to Dorothea for his workaholic ways and his overbearing ambition, a tacit admission that there were more important things in life than gold records. The confident and mature handling of this song was a sharp contrast to the cumbersome 'Silent Night' from *7800 Degrees Fahrenheit*. It also illustrated just how far Jon had progressed from the days when he had crassly proclaimed that any woman that came between him and his guitar would not last five minutes.

How much of *Keep The Faith* was a calculated adjustment to the band's profile and how much a heartfelt change in attitude is one of the great imponderables. Certainly Jon performed the material with sincerity and seemed genuinely to believe in the new ideas that he was trying to articulate. Some critics felt that he had advanced the cause of Bon Jovi, Stuart Clark in *Hot Press* suggesting that the album was 'hardly the musical reinvention that's been promised but neither is it the sound of a band merely going through the motions . . . "Dry County" is probably their trump card, a ten minute epic which bemoans the pitiful state of middle America with unexpected eloquence.' It was Adam Sweeting in the *Guardian* who most accurately caught the prevailing view among the musical *cognoscenti* however: 'the band's legendary love of clichés survives unimpaired but they nick some good clichés. One can never come right out and admit one likes Bon Jovi unless it's to one's therapist but they have a glaring gift for melodrama and cheap thrills.'

Therein lay the great Bon Jovi paradox; plenty of people loved their easy way with a singable chorus but few were willing to admit to the unfashionable sin of actually liking a band that had such a mindless image. Anton Corbijn's photographic work had helped them to address that dichotomy but it was always likely to be a long haul to respectability. If one wanted proof of Jon's integrity, it was in those pictures.

Looking at the *Slippery* photo shoots, here was a singer with nothing in his eyes except a youthful, roguish sparkle. Slapping on a plastic smile and a plastic expression to sell posters and records all over the world, there was no depth to his features, no indication that he had seen anything of the world, no hint that he was anything other than a young pop star riding his luck. When you spent time with Corbijn's work, you could see that Jon no longer had the glazed expression of the cat that got the cream. Frivolity had been replaced with the penetrating stare of a man with a purpose. The lines around the eyes spoke of a character who had experienced much in a short time, emotions that were intrinsic and extrinsic to him. Here was a serious writer with something to say and yet here too was a confused young man, uncertain of where the next few years might lead him. His life had brought him into contact with people and situations that were alien to him; he had new stories to tell with his music, stories for which he did not yet have all the words. Corbijn's photos caught him reaching out for that new lexicon and yet there was a suspicion of doubt, questions about his viability in this new arena, concerns about the possible loss of his hard won position on top of the musical tree. Perhaps this is merely throwing weight on to an empty vessel, the consequence of interpreting anything through the genius of Corbijn's work, but it is in that interpretation of his subjects that his genius lies. He photographs what is really there rather than what a stylist would like you to see. As the title of the next album would imply, Jon stood at the crossroads of his career with *Keep The Faith*.

American audiences were slow to warm to this new incarnation, the album only reaching number five on the Billboard survey though 'Bed Of Roses' did reach the Top Ten singles chart. Neverthless, *Keep The Faith* ultimately totalled eight million sales world-wide, which was pretty healthy by any standards except their own. Part of this comparative failure lay in the change of musical emphasis from crowd-pleasing anthems to songs that empathized with an underprivileged section of American society, pointing an accusing finger at the rest. The biggest reason that those extra two or three million units remained unshifted was Jon's refusal to subject himself to the kind of touring timetable that had wrecked the band in the first place, indicating that he was serious about stretching himself musically rather than commercially.

This time around, Bon Jovi embarked on a rather more manageable six-month trek around the world, ending with another outdoor bonanza at the Milton Keynes Bowl, the group having long since outgrown the confines of the Donington festival. Jon's attitude was coloured by memories of the final few shows of the *New Jersey* tour. Looking back on those post-Christmas gigs in England, he explained:

> Brian May and Elton John came onstage with us at Wembley ... I wasn't enjoying it, I was too busy thinking about the next show. Brian's smart and I think he recognized the symptoms. He told me to enjoy each day as it came. He felt that his own years with Queen had flown by ... now I'm living for the moment and loving every second. If I'm burned out on the road, I'm going to know it this time.

Precautions were taken to prevent such problems from arising. Even though they were compressing the touring into a shorter period, they ensured that every now and again there was provision for a few days off, allowing the band to go to the beach, rest and relax. Financially it wasn't such a good idea, but what's money for if not to squander? The shows were all the better for the relaxed attitude, as Stuart Clark told the *Hot Press* readership: 'Bon Jovi go all the way − what separates them from the rest of the stadium metal posse is their inherent ability to write a memorable tune and then milk it for all its theatrical worth. Entertainment with a capital E.' Certainly the live show was not a radical departure in any sense, for Jon, quite legitimately, felt that people parting with their money for a concert deserved a damned good night out. If he wanted to make them think a little harder about themselves and their world, a record was the best place for that particular task.

The happiest event of the tour came on a personal note when Dorothea gave birth to their first daughter, Stephanie Rose, on 31 May, which Jon termed 'the most amazing experience of my life. In fact it's addictive. Now I want ten more.' Dorothea's response to that did not go on record, but the birth gave rise to countless stories which portrayed Jon as the reformed wildman of rock. Certainly he had changed, as *Keep The Faith* had shown only too clearly, but one might not have expected him to say 'Fatherhood is exciting, a lot of fun'. The newly mellowed Jon Bon Jovi had learnt the lessons of the past, for there was no headlong dash back into the studio once touring duties were over, though stockpiling of material went on, with forty songs ready for work. Recording was slated to begin in January 1993 with Bob Rock, but such was the demand for Rock's services that the sessions had to be postpponed, Rock eventually being replaced by Peter Collins, who had previously worked with Rush and Gary Moore. Recording finally got under way in October 1994.

Jon did not remain idle through the year, however, for he took a featured role in the film *Moonlight And Valentino*, starring Whoopi Goldberg, Elizabeth Perkins and Kathleen Turner. Realistic about his limitations, Jon had taken acting lessons in preparation for the part but was still honest enough to admit to *Hot Press* that 'hopefully if I ever get out of my depth someone will say "Jon this sucks!" but it'll probably happen too late and I'll make a fool of myself'. At the time of writing, the film has yet to make it to the screen, so judgement has to be reserved on that front.

Jon came back to Bon Jovi refreshed, though later than expected. That being so, the record company had decided that a greatest hits package was required to fill the gap between albums. Initially against the idea, Jon was swayed by the way in which it could be used to ring down the curtain on the first chapter of Bon Jovi's career, clearing the way to usher in new music that was a further departure from their formulaic days of *Slippery When Wet*. Two new songs were commissioned for the album: 'Always', another of their epic ballads which became one of the top ten selling singles of the year in the UK, and 'Someday I'll Be Saturday Night', grittier fare in the lyrical mould of 'Keep The Faith'. Interestingly, on their release as singles, each was accompanied by a promotional video that barely featured the band at all, further indication of Jon's desire to withdraw from the spotlight.

If these two songs rounded off that first phase for Bon Jovi, the era was closed in another sense with the band's first real line-up change. In January 1994, Alec Jon Such announced that he did not want to play on the forthcoming album but that he would still be available for touring duties. This was something of a bombshell to the band's following, but it was no real surprise that after a decade or so someone was finally pulling in a different direction. Once Alec made it clear that he would not be touring either, Jon simply put the decision down to the fact that he had been round the world once too often and wanted to slow down and enjoy the money he had earned, as well as getting involved in other projects, including the managerial side of the business. As a man by now in his early forties, the idea of going from one hotel room to another had lost a little of its attraction.

This was contrary to several interviews that Alec did with the British press, where he was quite vociferous in his complaints, although he later protested that he had been taken out of context. The articles suggested that Jon treated him as an unimportant sideman, had told him that his playing wasn't up to scratch and that no-one in the press was interested in talking to him. Jon naturally denied these charges and, given that Such was with the group when they flew into the UK in September for a *Top Of The Pops* appearance to promote 'Always', there seemed to be no hard feelings between the two. On that same visit, Jon and Richie played a short, thirty-minute acoustic set in Covent Garden in front of 5,000 people alerted to the event by local radio and press.

One such charge that did strike a chord though; Jon and Richie were always looking for hits rather than great music, an accusation that Jon had been at great pains to refute in the run-up to *Keep The Faith*. This minor argument did little to foster the impression of harmony within the Bon Jovi camp, but it now appears to have been little more than a short squall. Such has not been replaced in the band, so it is possible that he might return to the fold in years to come. In the interim, Huey McDonald has been playing bass on the upcoming new album, having played on the original version of 'Runaway' back in 1982. He also performed with the band at their Christmas benefit shows. To mark their fifth year of these special gigs, they played five shows in total in December 1994 in Montreal,

Boston, Pittsburgh, Atlanta and the Count Basie Theater in Red Bank, New Jersey.

The compilation *Cross Road* exceeded expectations everywhere; in the UK it sold more than one and a half million copies, in America it was selling at a rate of one million per week and it went on to top virtually every chart in the world. This highly successful spell was concluded in the UK with the seasonal release of 'Please Come Home For Christmas'. Issued as a benefit single in aid of the Special Olympics charity, it was accompanied by a steamy video. Supermodel Cindy Crawford provided the love interest, though the timing could have been better, since the clip was released just after she had gone through her very public split with actor Richard Gere. The press put two and two together and made five, suggesting that Jon was now dating Ms Crawford, oblivious to the fact that he was shortly to become a father for the second time – a son was born in February 1995. Jon's reaction to the whole furore was simple: 'When I heard [about the video] I just said "I get to kiss Cindy Crawford for seven hours? Fine!"' The video did its job; the single was another hit and it put some much-needed money into the charity's coffers.

The end of 1994 found Jon at the crossroad. The choice of future is his; he can either take the lessons of the greatest hits album on board and churn out an endless series of 'Bad Medicine' clones to his financial advantage or he can continue the process of artistic growth that was signposted by *Keep The Faith*. Jon Bon Jovi has a truly great record inside him, one that he has yet to make. Only time will tell if he is willing to make the necessary commitment.

10

ITALIANAMERICAN

The history of rock'n'roll is littered with casualties of one kind or another. That more than anything else is what gives it its bohemian appeal and allows us to pretend that it is still an art form operating at the cutting edge of society – an increasingly vain belief. In reality, expecting anything 'dangerous' or 'subversive' from popular music these days is at best optimistic, at worst absurd. Rock'n'roll has been going for far too long now for the Establishment to fear it. Indeed most of the rock outlaws of the past have joined the very Establishment they professed to despise.

Perhaps it was the 1980s that put that myth to rest once and for all. The 1980s were the decade of technological advancement, of the compact disc and of the promotional video. It was a decade more than any other in pop's short history where the sole reason for the existence of a music industry seemed to be the creation of vast amounts of money for a few short-lived performers, the long-term benefits accruing to the shareholders.

Few bands seemed to personify this lust for success more expansively than Bon Jovi. In the middle of it all stood Jon Bon Jovi, the singer and songwriter who gave the group an identity, understandably enough since it was initially formed as a vehicle for his talents. Seemingly awash with self-confidence, Jon was brash and bold, he held audiences rapt with attention yet only dealt in the broadest of emotions, the most obvious of platitudes. To maximize their profit potential, he and his band were worked to the point of frenzy, pushed on to stage after stage in country after country long after their minds had ceased to function properly in the desperate search for extra dollars.

Somewhere, Jon and his colleagues managed to maintain a modicum of self-respect in this orgy of capitalism. From deep within, Jon and his writing partner Richie Sambora were able to dredge up songs that started to suggest that all was not well with Bon Jovi.

In a very different time, in a very different band, John Lennon wrote a song entitled 'Help!'. At the time it was regarded as nothing more than the theme tune to a knockabout musical comedy film but when critics began to dissect the lyrics, as they eventually did, they found that John Lennon meant every last word. At the helm of the biggest, best, most important rock'n'roll band the world has ever seen, or will see, John Lennon was, almost unbelievably, asking for help. If Jon Bon Jovi possessed one half of Lennon's talent, he would stand above every musician playing today and would be hailed as a genius. There is no comparison between Lennon and Bon Jovi as songwriters; indeed Lennon has no equals in contemporary popular music. There is no shame in that for he was an iconoclast, a one-off who shaped the future of popular music in the company of his fellow Beatles – and let's face it, Richie Sambora is no Paul McCartney either. Where the comparisons are relevant is in terms of the success they enjoyed – or at least achieved – and the demands it made on them as people.

It is greatly to Jon's credit that he was finally able to come out of the other side of the experience as a much improved songwriter, a better man, husband and father; many others have not been so fortunate, tenacious or just downright lucky. His roots, his experience as an Italian American have stood him in good stead. The values of loyalty and devotion to his closest family and friends enabled him to turn the inner core of Bon Jovi into a shell that protected the individual members from the intrusions of the voracious media and industry.

His background also helped him keep his feet on the ground and only very rarely did he allow himself to be sucked into the glamorous world of popular entertainment. Michael Jackson, Prince and Madonna are victims of their own celebrity, creating a self-fulfilling prophecy of stardom that imprisons them in their own homes or hotel rooms. Jon has had no truck with that nonsense. He still goes to football games, he still walks the streets. So he has to sign a few autographs on the way. So what? Wisely he argues,

I've always thought the greatest fallacy was 'I'm a prisoner of rock'n'roll' . . . I'll never become a prisoner . . . I know where I come from, we just think we're lucky to have a great job that makes people happy . . . it's as sane as you wanna make it . . . it's not like limousines and entourages. It never was and it never will be . . . any time you think that because you're in a rock band that you're anything more than the guy in the front row, you lose. It's bullshit.

Such common sense is a rare commodity among those who can legitimately be termed 'superstars', but in his business it's the greatest gift. Maybe that has been Jon's biggest achievement, that he remained a decent individual – not faultless by any means as this book has shown, but not a monster or a drug-addled mess, the fate mapped out for so many stars. He's a paradox certainly and some of his statements are those of a man a little too wrapped up in himself to realize that he's being pretentious or just talking complete rubbish. For instance: 'The toys are a Ferrari, a couple of Corvettes, a couple of Jeeps and a couple of Harleys which I hardly ever get to drive . . . I'm not materialistic.' Not materialistic no, but obviously a very poor shopper. But if that's the worst that can be said of someone who has made it to the very top of his profession, it's quite a recommendation.

What the future holds for Bon Jovi is anyone's guess. Certainly with two children in tow, Jon is likely to cut back on the workload that he attacked so energetically seven or eight years ago, but then he no longer needs to work that hard, such was his success. He looks likely to age gracefully with a renewed musical purpose about him. Jon has left the world of heavy rock a long way behind him. He's no longer trapped in the tragic cartoon world where rather sad caricatures like Aerosmith stalk girls young enough to be their daughters, almost their granddaughters, with their testosterone-injected rock clichés. With those days behind him, perhaps Jon can earn and receive the respect he so patently craves.

His songwriting has come on significantly from the earliest days of *Bon Jovi*, yet he is still condemned as a mindless populist. In live performance, he makes no secret of the fact that he wants to enjoy the show and wants people to come along to the gigs: 'What I try and do is have as much fun as I can, get a bar atmosphere going. When I look around an arena. I want everybody standing. If people are sitting on their hands they're not having a good time.' Not an especially cerebral attitude but a warm-hearted one that some acts could do worse than copy.

Bon Jovi were designed for popularity and that's a goal they will always pursue, to a greater or lesser degree. It is to be hoped that the future will see them willing to experiment further with their sound, though Jon's commercial instincts will always leave him rooted in the mainstream. Since 'mainstream' is just a clever way of saying 'popular', perhaps it's time to stop using that as a pejorative and revel in its positive aspect – the idea of celebration and of bringing people together: 'As a kid that was never my idea of being in rock band, to play to half an arena. The sound of empty seats is not one I care to hear.'

If you can turn 'mainstream' on its head and use it to your advantage it can also be an honest course, for as Jon proclaimed, 'If you don't want kids to love your stuff and buy it then what are you in this business for?' Some might find that crassly commercial. Certainly it does not pay sufficient respect to the claims of many fine artists for whom expressing themselves is more important than any other consideration. Yet it misses the point of Bon Jovi. They were created for popular consumption, to appeal to kids all over the world. They make no bones about it and have made a lot of people very happy in the process. That's not such a bad epitaph, though Jon might choose a different one. The last word is his: 'Experience man, there's nothing like it.'

SOURCES

The following publications have all been of the greatest value. It is not a definitive list of the material consulted and not all have been quoted from in the text, but all were particularly useful nonetheless.

DAILY EXPRESS:
'Don't Call Me A Pin-Up' by David Wigg, 22 August 1987.

DAILY MAIL:
'Confessions Of A Bimboy' by Chrissy Iley, 23 August 1989.
'Showdown For "Cowboy" Jon' by Spencer Bright, 11 November 1992.

DAILY MIRROR:
'A Walk On The Mild Side' by Rachel Loos, 8 September 1993.

DAILY STAR:
'Drugs Killed My Friends' by Rick Sky, 10 September 1986.

THE GUARDIAN:
'Metal's Mettle' by Adam Sweeting, 2 December 1988.
'Candy Floss Rock' by Adam Sweeting, 4 January 1990.
Blaze of Glory LP review by Adam Sweeting, 9 August 1990.
Keep The Faith LP review by Adam Sweeting, 30 October 1992.
'Search For A New Faith' by Caroline Sullivan, 6 November 1992.

HOT PRESS:
Keep The Faith LP review by Stuart Clark, 2 December 1992.
Live review, Dublin Point by Stuart Clark, 16 June 1993.
'Bon Voyage' by Stuart Clark, 22 September 1993.

MELODY MAKER:
'Bon Voyages' by Carol Clerk, 25 May 1985.
'Overnight Sensation' by Carol Clerk, 13 September 1986.
Live review, Hammersmith Odeon by Carol Clerk, 29 November 1986.
New Jersey LP review by Carol Clerk, 24 September 1988.
'Hand To Mouth' by Carol Clerk, 2 September 1989.
'The Beloved Entertainer' by The Stud Brothers, 16 December 1989.

NEW MUSICAL EXPRESS:
'Yankee Noodle Dandies' by Simon Witter, 24 December 1988.
'Bon In The USA' by Stuart Maconie, 2 September 1989.
'The Fifth Most Famous Man In Rock' by Andrew Collins, 16 December 1989.

NEWS OF THE WORLD:
'Bon Jovi Rules OK' by Gill Pringle, 2 May 1993.

Q:
'Rock'n'roll! It's A Bitch!' by Adrian Deevoy, November 1987.
New Jersey LP review by Marc Cooper, November 1988.
'If You've Got It, Flaunt It!' by Adrian Deevoy, January 1989.
Blaze Of Glory LP review by Barry McIlheney, September 1990.
'The Right Trousers' by Andrew Collins, November 1994.
'I Believe In America' by David Cavanagh, February 1995.

ROLLING STONE:
'Bon Voyage' by Rob Tannenbaum, 9 February 1989.
Reprinted by permission of Straight Arrow Publishers, Inc. 1989.
All rights reserved.

SELECT:
'Shootin' 'Em Dead In Hollywood' by Mark Putterford, September 1990.

SMASH HITS:
'I Am Superman!' by Tom Hibbert, 8 April 1987.
'Personal File', 9 August 1989.
'Come In! Meet The Wife!' by Steve Beebee, 15 February 1995.

SOUNDS:
Bon Jovi LP review by Jay Williams, 21 April 1984.
'Bon Appetit' by Robbi Millar, 7 July 1984.
'Hot Shots' by Robbi Millar, 11 May 1985.
'Bon Voyage' by Robbi Millar, 23 August 1986.
'Is Jon Bon Jovi A Sex God?' by Neil Perry, 10 January 1987.
'Livin' On A Bus' by Richard Cook, 22 August 1987.
'Hometown Boys' by Paul Elliott, 10 September 1988.
'Firewater From the Medicine Men' by Paul Elliott, 17 September 1988.
'Alias Ron And Reg' by Paul Elliott, 29 April 1989.
'Greetings From Gorky Park' by Neil Perry, 19 August 1989.
'The French Connection' by Mary Anne Hobbs, 16 December 1989.
'Back In The Saddle' by Paul Elliott, 4 August 1990.

SUNDAY MIRROR:
'Cher's Bon Boys' by Robin Eggar, 13 December 1992.
'I Bought A House, Three Mercs . . .' by Sally Beck, 16 May 1993.
'Très Bon Jovi' by Stephen Eastwood, 5 September 1993.

SUNDAY TIMES:
'A Life In The Day Of Jon Bon Jovi' by Linda O'Keeffe, 9 May 1993.

THE TIMES:
'It Sells But Is It Really Any Good?' by Steve Turner, 29 December 1989.

163

HOW TO ORDER YOUR TITLES FROM BOXTREE

MUSIC

1-85283-553-2	Carpenters: Untold Story	£15.99 hb
0-7522-1665-1	Carpenters: Untold Story	£7.99 pb
0-7522-0824-1	The Complete NME Album Charts	£9.99 pb
0-7522-0829-2	The Complete NME Singles Charts	£9.99 pb
0-7522-1697-X	The Country 1035 am Encyclopedia of American Country Music	£16.99 hb
0-7522-0842-X	Metallica	£4.99 pb
0-7522-0627-3	REM Documental	£8.99 pb
1-85283-877-3	Rolling Stones – Images of the World Tour	£9.99 pb
1-85283-396-3	Take That: On the Road	£5.99 pb
0-7522-0988-4	Take That: Under my Pillow	£5.99 pb
0-7522-0835-7	U2: Wide Awake in America	£4.99 pb
0-7522-0989-2	Who Killed Christopher Robin: Life	£14.99 hb

All these books are available at your local bookshop or can be ordered direct from the publisher. Just tick the titles you want and fill in the form below.

Prices and availability subject to change without notice.

Boxtree Cash Sales, P.O. Box 11, Falmouth, Cornwall TR10 9EN

Please send a cheque or postal order for the value of the book and add the following for postage and packing:

U.K. including B.F.P.O. – £1.00 for one book plus 50p for the second book, and 30p for each additional book ordered up to a £3.00 maximum.

Overseas including Eire – £2.00 for the first book plus £1.00 for the second book, and 50p for each additional book ordered.

OR please debit this amount from my Access/Visa Card (delete as appropriate).

Card Number ☐☐☐☐☐☐☐☐☐☐☐☐☐☐☐☐

Amount £ ....

Expiry Date ....

Signed ....

Name ....

Address ....